STEPPING OUTSIDE THE SECRETS

This book celebrates the stren͟g  ꞇct
of great courage to commit t͟ ꞌp
outside our secrets is perhaps ꞇaul (yoga)
toward becoming a fully fre͟ ꞇ.ꞇ.ꞇually evolved person.
Through her life and shared experience, Dr. Hodge models this
path. Besides a fascinating read, the reader will find in her book
a compelling invitation to enter their own journey of self-
discovery.
Allyn Roberts, Ph.D., Director, Clinical Services, Omega
Psychology Center

A gut-wrenching and inspiring story of a psychologist's journey
from severe sexual abuse to spiritual awareness. Hodge's search
ranges from exploration of past lives and Native American
spirituality to the 12-step program and ancient philosophies,
leading her to peace, forgiveness, love and service. A compelling
and engrossing story filled with twists and turns that kept me
reading.
Palma Richardson, author, *I Remember Alice*

One woman's courageous awakening from a pattern of sexual
abuse initiated by her father. In recounting her story, Dr. Hodge
provides her readers with a guidebook to self-acceptance and
forgiveness. Highly recommended.
Caron Goode, Ed.D., author, *Nurture Your Child's Gift: Inspired
Parenting*

Stepping Outside the Secrets

A Spiritual Journey from
Sexual Abuse to Inner Peace

Stepping Outside the Secrets

A Spiritual Journey from Sexual Abuse to Inner Peace

Elaine A. Hodge

BOOKS

Winchester, UK
Washington, USA

First published by O-Books, 2015
O-Books is an imprint of John Hunt Publishing Ltd., Laurel House, Station Approach,
Alresford, Hants, SO24 9JH, UK
office1@jhpbooks.net
www.johnhuntpublishing.com

For distributor details and how to order please visit the 'Ordering' section on our website.

ISBN: 978 1 78279 789 0
Library of Congress Control Number: 2014944849

A CIP catalogue record for this book is available from the British Library.

Design: Lee Nash

Printed and bound by CPI Group (UK) Ltd, Croydon, CR0 4YY

We operate a distinctive and ethical publishing philosophy in all
areas of our business, from our global network of authors to
production and worldwide distribution.

CONTENTS

The author of this book does not dispense medical advice or prescribe the use of any technique as a form of treatment for physical, medical or mental health problems without the advice of a physician and/or mental health professional. This book reflects the author's experiences, knowledge and expertise; the information, advice and instruction are provided for educational purposes and general reference only and are not intended as a substitute for medical advice or counseling. The author, publisher and distributor are not responsible in any manner for any injury or liability that may result from practicing – or attempting to practice – the techniques described herein.

Some of the names and identifying details in this book have been changed to protect the privacy of individuals, but all the stories are real and true.

To the Creator, the Source, the Divine Within —
and to all the women whose spirits have been wounded
by sexual abuse.

Introduction

There is no agony like bearing an untold story inside of you.
Maya Angelou

For years, I've held an untold story within me and was imprisoned by the shame of it. I have come through the dark tunnel of sexual abuse and found the light at the other end. Like other molested women before me, I held so tightly to the story that I would almost rather die than admit the shame that Daddy's fondling was not because he cherished his daughter but because he was a pathetic, abusive, alcoholic child molester.

That was the beginning.

My sexual abuse that started in childhood continued through my adolescent and early adult years. My first abuser, my alcoholic father, began sexually fondling me when I was five. As I look back, I wonder what signals or signs alerted other predators that I was available. At age nine, my brother's friend sexually abused me for two years. While attending Catholic schools, I endured inappropriate sexual talk and behavior from two Catholic priests. At thirteen, my dentist sexually molested me, and when I was seventeen my first boss took advantage of me sexually. At twenty-one, I was raped by my second boss.

Someone was hurt before you . . . beaten before you; humiliated before you; raped before you; yet someone survived.
Maya Angelou

My story is unique in that I survived, forgave my abusers, and found an inner resilience that allowed me to take charge of my life when I couldn't explain to myself why my relationships were not working. Not everyone survives. Every two minutes someone, most likely a white, female child, is sexually abused or raped by someone close to her, most likely a relative.[1] The long-term effects of childhood sexual abuse are all-encompassing, affecting many aspects of a victim's life – relationships, intimacy, work, self-esteem and emotionality. Women who are sexually abused as a child are more likely to develop a drug or alcohol dependency. Seventy-five percent of women in treatment programs for drug and alcohol abuse report having been sexually abused.[2]

The choice to retake control of a life after sexual abuse, to move from victimhood to empowerment, happens when one becomes aware of the dysfunctional patterns that repeat themselves in one's existence. For me it involved recognizing that I chose one alcoholic relationship after another and continually subjected myself to additional emotional and sexual abuse, always hoping the new man might give me the love I never received from my father.

I kept searching for someone to ease my pain and fill the emptiness inside, but that never happened. After my last disastrous relationship with a married alcoholic, I hit bottom. I had to admit that my life was a mess and I needed help. I crawled into the room of a twelve-step recovery meeting, desperate for answers. In the years that followed, I found those answers in recovery rooms, in a therapist's office, and in my spiritual journey.

God gave us the gift of life: it is up to us to give ourselves the gift of living well.
Voltaire

In Native American philosophy, sometimes the wounded victim finds healing by understanding the wounding event in the scheme of her life-purpose and by learning how to take the gift she has been offered and share it with others. The pain of my early abuse forced me to dive deep into my spiritual self for comfort and eventually to study psychology to understand my father.

Today, I see that my life-purpose and work evolved from the very circumstances that I found so painful to endure at the time.

I also learned that deep in the memory of the wounding is the memory of the survival technique or tool that helped me to be resilient. A part of each victim knows how to survive and not be crushed, and each of us has to find that tool for healing. My resilience was built by asking questions: *Why did this happen to me? What could I learn from it?* Since I believed in God, in the larger scheme of things I asked a bigger question: *What am I here to do?* The wounded, those who suffer, need to know that such experiences are not in vain, so that healing at all levels can occur.

I found out that the abuse that happened to me was not as important as how I handled it. I decided not to be a victim and be beaten down by adversity. I made a proactive choice to heal. I discovered that I could learn from my experiences and not drown in self-pity. I learned how to love others as well as myself more deeply through recovery and therapy. I learned how to set healthy boundaries and not put up with abuse. I discovered how to live a happy and fulfilling life without needing another person to fix me. I learned how to forgive.

Once I learned from the experiences, the natural outgrowth was service, which comes naturally to me. I became an advocate for child protection and counseled women who were recovering from abuse. I developed a meaningful and strong relationship with a Higher Power and found my Self through an exploration of profound, life-changing spiritual paths. I began doing spiritual counseling and healing energy work with others and began conducting spiritual workshops and teaching meditation.

As a wounded woman, I have something important to give to the world: the story of my journey and recovery. I share that journey with you in this book. My wish is that others who have been sexually abused will find hope through my story and also survive, thrive, and find a deep love for themselves and satisfaction in all they become.

Part I

Abuse

Childhood sexual abuse results in the loss of self-identity,
connection with others, trust, faith, reality, security and control.[3]
Cara L. Stiles, MSW

I

The Beginning

Oh no! That sound again! The wailing of the neighbor's dog, outside in a chain link kennel full of dog poop and dirty water, totally neglected. Beaten down by the hard rain, wind, hail and snow, Buddy and his lonely existence seemed to be noticed by no one but me. I cringed every time I heard his intermittent cries, each pitiful howl sinking my heart deeper and deeper into sadness. I wanted to rescue him, take him away, hold him in my arms, and tell him I loved him; but I was powerless. My own dog, Spirit, a beautiful and healthy dark-red golden retriever, lay beside me on his comfortable cedar bed. In response to his puzzled look I crouched down, enfolded him in my arms, and gave him a comforting hug, transferring loving energy to the wretched pup outside.

In an attempt to help, I called Animal Control; they did nothing except make the owner clean up the piles of poop. The next morning my disheveled hillbilly neighbor banged on my front door, his face red with rage, and screamed that I'd be sorry if I didn't stay out of his business. Buddy – such an ironic name – emitted another long, mournful wail, like someone grieving the loss of a loved one. Choking back tears and welling up with fury, I entertained thoughts of stealing the dog and killing my neighbor.

For two years I agonized over Buddy and wondered why he bothered me so. Staring out the back window, I watched him pace back and forth in his tiny cage with no way out, wanting to comfort him, to reassure him he was not alone. Then one day it hit me. His pain was a reflection of my own suffering growing up in an abusive, alcoholic home. Like Buddy, I too was trapped with nowhere to go and no one to rescue me. I knew what it was like to be alone in a living hell!

I was five. Dad sat in his overstuffed, dirty green chair reeking of alcohol, puffing on a cigar, filling the warm room with a stinky blue-gray haze that made it difficult to breathe, while Mom scurried around the house like a scared rabbit, trying to meet everyone's demands. Sitting with his unbuckled belt and unzipped fly, Daddy called me to his lap. At first I was excited as I leaped into his outstretched arms. *He's paying attention to me!* I loved my daddy and hungered for his love in return as I cuddled in his protective arms. Resting there, I felt everything would be okay.

But it wasn't, for soon my life changed forever.

One evening, Dad patted his lap and said, "Come here, honey!" He put his arm around me, rubbed my slim shoulder, stroked my blond hair, and told me, "You're my special little girl." I lay in his big strong arms, soaking up his attention, trying to ignore the stinky cigar in his hand and the smell of alcohol on his breath. To be close to Daddy meant I had to put up with all his foul smells.

As we sat alone in the living room watching *The Lone Ranger,* my dad's favorite show, he rubbed my stomach and then slipped his hand under my shorts and panties and touched my pee-pee. I froze! *What is he doing? What if someone sees us? It doesn't feel right.* I wiggled to get off his lap, but he held me tight and whispered in my ear, "It's okay, honey. Daddy loves you." *Does that make what he's doing okay? I don't know. I'm confused. I want him to love me. Is this love? It must be all right then.* I sat still, letting him touch me, but deep down I felt yucky in my gut. Something was wrong. All I wanted was Daddy's love and attention – and to get it I had to put up with his rough, rubbing hands.

Each night, when I heard my father's old yellow Ford Fairlane pull into the driveway, my heart raced and my shoulders tensed up. *Will he touch me again? Will he start a fight?* I knew he'd be drunk, but how drunk would he be, and who would he pick on tonight? Usually it was Mom, but Jeff, the oldest, was also one of his favorite targets, and he didn't hesitate to use his leather belt on the rest of us. *Why doesn't he just stay away? Everyone is happier when he's not around.*

He came into the house and Mom got in his face and screamed, "Oh no, John, you've been drinking again," as if it were a surprise. "Shut up!" he said, as he brushed her aside and staggered to his chair. Mom followed him, shouting, "I thought you were going to stop drinking." Dad lifted his right hand and backhanded Mom hard on her right shoulder. "Get out of here."

Sorrowfully, I watched my mother run crying into the kitchen. I hated him. I wanted to hit him back, but I sat silently on the couch, not moving a muscle, trying to be invisible, my stomach in knots, afraid for my own safety and feeling guilty that I could not protect Mom.

Soon it was dinnertime, accompanied by the tension that was always present when Dad was around and drunk. My stomach began doing its usual flip-flops, hunger mixing with fear. You could always count on a big drama unfolding at the table. Dad didn't want to eat and cut the high from his buzz, so he'd start complaining that his steak was undercooked while the rest of us sat staring at the hamburger on our plate. Mom jumped up like the puppet she was around Dad, rushed to the kitchen, cooked the meat some more, hurried back, and placed it in front of him. He picked at it like it was poison, snarled, "It's still not right," and stormed away from the table in a huff, leaving us all upset.

Mom cried, groveling and offering apologies to Dad for her cooking, which made me angry. *Why can't she see what he's doing? It isn't her cooking. He just doesn't want to eat.* I hurt when I saw her trying so hard to please him. I wanted to scream, "Stop it, Mom, it's not your fault!" but I knew it wouldn't do any good. Dad had already brainwashed her into thinking she was to blame.

I liked Mom's cooking. She made great meals like meatloaf,

mashed potatoes, and string beans, and her delicious homemade chili. Sometimes, she surprised me by baking a cherry pie, my favorite dessert. She'd whisper in my ear, "I made this just for you." I'd smile my biggest smile, feeling so special.

I hated the fighting, but at the same time I felt sorry for my father. He drove a big oil truck all day to support the family. Why couldn't he have a few drinks after work? But what did I, a child of five, know about such things? I couldn't understand the dilemma of a mother overwhelmed with too much responsibility, unpaid bills, and a drunken husband.

Our house sat on a tree-lined street in a mid to upper-class neighborhood in Covington, Kentucky. It was an attractive two-story, red brick home with potted deep-red geraniums lining the porch railing. An old wooden swing, painted pea green, hung by heavy chains from the porch ceiling, a favorite spot to sit on hot summer nights. The house was surrounded by two giant oak trees, which provided a canopy of shade in the sweltering Kentucky summers and an abundant supply of acorns for the hungry chipmunks and squirrels.

Inside the front door was a rectangular-shaped living room with a couple of stuffed chairs and a couch flanked by two end tables, each with a lamp. A beautifully crafted wood mantel rested atop the fireplace, with built-in bookcases on each end. Through the arched doorway to the left was the dining room, where we gathered for family meals around a large oval-shaped oak table. Behind the dining room was the kitchen, Mom's room, with its brightly painted yellow cabinets and matching yellow window valances.

At the top of the staircase leading to the second floor was my room – the girls' room – sparsely decorated with a small dresser, double bed and daybed, just enough room for me and my two sisters to sleep in. Down the hallway on the left was our only bathroom, quite a challenge for a family of ten. At the end of the hallway were two more nondescript bedrooms. The boys' room, to the right, had two double beds for my four brothers. My parents' room, on the left, held a double bed plus the baby bed for my youngest sister.

Behind the house there was an extended driveway with a basketball court. Up a small embankment filled with orange tiger lilies was a spacious backyard with a swing and plenty of room for touch football games. Everything looked idyllic from the outside. But inside, the walls guarded well-kept secrets, and skeletons hid in the closets: dark secrets of sexual abuse, hard, heavy drinking, and violence.

Mom was a hardy woman of German heritage who believed strongly in hard work and religious devotion. Being a devout Catholic, she did not practice birth control, so the babies rolled out like cars off an assembly line. I was the fifth child in six years, followed by three more. I liked being in a large family and having lots of brothers and sisters to play with. I don't remember Mom ever holding me on her lap, hugging or kissing me, or even telling me she loved me; but somehow I knew she did.

Once it began, my father's sexual touching continued, apparently with no one in our crowded home paying attention. Then one day my mother came around the corner, saw me sitting on his lap, and screamed, "Elaine, get down! You're too big to be sitting on your father's lap!" I jumped down, feeling as if I'd done something terribly wrong. *It's my fault. I'm to blame. I'm a bad person.*

Looking back, I see how I took on the blame, as many abused children do. When we are young, our vision of the world is small, and everything is about us: what we do or don't do. *If I hadn't said that, this wouldn't have happened. If I hadn't done that, everybody would have been happy.* The tendency to self-reference is what makes it so easy for a young child to pick up blame. Young children do not possess the mental skills necessary to refute the erroneous idea that they are to blame and to see that there is no truth to it. I repeatedly told myself that if I hadn't sat on Daddy's lap it wouldn't have happened. It was *my* fault, and I carried that shame for years – until I realized it was only natural for a child to want to be close to her father and want his love. I did nothing wrong!

There are many other reasons why children grow up blaming themselves for sexual abuse. Sometimes they feel it's their fault for not trying harder to stop it, for not saying no, or for not telling anyone, even if their perpetrator said it was a secret or threatened harm if they told someone. If a child experienced abuse from multiple abusers who are not related, she might feel that it's her fault because there were so many. This is what happened to me. There were multiple abusers, and because I was the one constant in the picture I felt there must be something wrong with *me*. Some children feel guilty because it felt good or they were sexually aroused, which is natural.

The shame and blame that is picked up by a sexually abused child creates a veil of secrecy. You can't tell anyone because you assume it's your fault, and that would make you a bad person. There is a saying that we are only as sick as our secrets, and this is especially true with childhood sexual abuse. Part of the healing involves getting the bogeyman out of the closet, talking about the secrets, and coming to the realization that we are victims. A child can never ever be to blame for sexual abuse.

The sexual abuse at the hands of my father marked the beginning of my confusion between sex and love. The two intermingled, with love and sex being one and the same. For many years I struggled with setting healthy sexual boundaries with men, continually unable to say no. I found myself perpetually thinking that if I went along with sex, I would get love. Yet, that never happened. I ended up feeling used and abused. Finally, I realized that sex is sex and love is love. In adult relationships, they sometimes go together. Sexual abuse, however, is never about love. My dad and others who abused me didn't love me. They stole my soul and stripped me of my dignity.

2

Catholicism and Shame

It was Friday, and I wakened to the sounds of birds chirping outside my open window. I lingered in bed, not wanting to get up, until it dawned on me that in two days I was going to make my First Holy Communion. My excitement at the thought propelled me out of bed like a jungle animal, eyes wide open, on full alert. I had to get ready for school, where Sister Lucille would go over the final instructions for Sunday.

On Saturday night Mom tied rags over all the bathroom faucets so I couldn't get up in the middle of the night and take a drink of water. In the early fifties the Catholic Church had strict fasting guidelines. Sister Lucille had told me, "You are forbidden to eat or drink anything after midnight if you want to receive Communion the next morning. If you break your fast and go to Communion, you commit a mortal sin. And if you die before going to Confession, you will go to hell." I certainly didn't want to go to hell, so I was glad Mom tied up all the faucets.

Finally it was Sunday! I got up and took a bath and Mom curled my hair. She dressed me in a beautiful white-laced dress with a gathered waist and ruffled hem, then placed on my head a long white veil that extended down to the middle of my back. White gloves and shiny white patent leather shoes completed my outfit. I looked and felt like a little porcelain doll.

In church, my family watched as I reverently approached the altar and received Jesus for the first time. The Church taught that Communion was the *actual* body and blood of Christ, so this was a special moment. I was so thrilled to meet Jesus in Communion that I thought my heart would burst. I bowed my head and said, "Jesus, I love you *so much*. Thank you for coming to be with me."

After Mom took pictures outside the church, we drove home

and friends and family began arriving for my party. I could hardly contain my excitement. They were coming to see me in my pretty white dress. I was the star of the show. Even some of my older brothers' and sisters' friends showed up. My oldest brother, Jeff, who was thirteen, invited his best friend Ronnie to drop by. Ronnie was a fixture at our house. He was like part of the family. When Ronnie saw me, he said, "Hi, Sweetie," and gave me a big hug. "Now don't you look pretty in your white dress?" Beaming a sunny smile, I politely said, "Thank you."

I liked Ronnie. His easy sense of humor made me laugh, and I especially appreciated that he paid special attention to me. It was both exciting and disturbing to watch how he and Jeff always managed to get into trouble together. I secretly observed them as they took a big swig of wine from the bottle for the guests on the kitchen table. Later, I saw them sneak outside behind the house to have a smoke. They were often up to no good.

The guests milled around me and made over my dress and gave me gifts: prayer books, rosaries, cards and money. Mom served her delicious deep-fried chicken, baked beans, potato salad, and chocolate cake. We had a feast. I fell into bed that evening exhausted but very much in high spirits.

The next day I left early for school to spend time on the playground before church. All our school days began with Mass and Communion. The bell rang. I came in hot and sweaty from playing and took a drink at the water fountain, something I had done every school day for two years. Not until I got to church did I realize I had broken my fast. I panicked and wondered which would be worse, committing a sin or telling Mom I didn't receive Communion. Confused and worried, I obsessed over my two options. When the time arrived, I just followed my other classmates to the altar and received Communion, but I knew I had to go to Confession the next day.

Along with First Communion came Confession, admitting our sins to the priest. Yikes! This was not half as exciting as receiving

Communion, but a good Catholic has to do it. Terrified, I went to Confession and confessed my sin: "Bless me, Father, for I have sinned, I broke my Communion fast." The priest replied, "What you did was just like spitting in the face of Jesus."

I was devastated. I felt so ashamed. Tears began pouring down my little seven-year-old cheeks. I mumbled through my Act of Contrition, left the confessional box, and ran out of church sobbing. *How could I have hurt Jesus? Surely, I am a bad person.* I had picked up the blame and carried guilt about my father touching me, and now I had hurt Jesus. Horrified, I felt I would carry the priest's harsh reprimand for as long as I lived, and I have never forgotten his response.

My self-esteem was already low, and the additional bashing by this priest heaped more shame on my tiny shoulders. Something shattered in me that day that I'd never be able to fix. I lost my innocence and truly believed I was a terrible person.

3

More Abuse

Over the next couple of years, I felt so lonely. Even though there were a lot of people around, everyone seemed enveloped in their own cocoon of personal pain. No one really talked to each other except to make sarcastic remarks or pick on someone. I couldn't tell anyone what I was thinking or feeling; it wasn't safe. I wondered why Mom or Dad didn't pay more attention to me. Mom busied herself with taking care of the babies and the house, while Dad was either at work or passed out drunk in his chair.

I thought back to when I was five and Mom caught me climbing up to the top of the kitchen cabinet. I had pushed a chair over to the counter and was scaling the shelves when she caught me. I was after a special treat: her hidden candy. Mom was trying to lose weight and had stored her diet-aid 'caramels' on the top shelf. She grabbed me, pulled me down, and angrily asked, "What are you doing?" I said, "I want to eat your candy so I can become little and you'll like me better than Randy [my baby brother]."

The next year, when I was six, it was *my* turn to get my picture taken on the back of a small black-and-white pony that a photographer brought through the neighborhood. The pony had white bows in its hair and a fancy saddle with bells and black ribbons. He was so pretty. In previous years my older brothers and sisters had all had their pictures taken on the pony, and now it was my turn to shine. I was up on the saddle, feeling so special, when my mother decided to move me behind the seat and place Randy in the saddle. I felt wounded with disappointment. *Why can't it just be me on the pony? It's my day!*

Although I didn't know it at the time, I was starving for attention: to feel special, to see myself as a lovable and worthwhile individual, to build up my self-esteem that had been damaged by my father's sexual abuse. Childhood sexual abuse results in a loss of self-identity. When a child experiences trauma, there needs to be someone there to hold her hand, to help her make sense out of the trauma so she can integrate it into her life. Without such support, she lacks a sense of trust, safety and well-being. Since most childhood sexual abuse is shrouded in secrecy, many children do not receive this support and become fragmented, split off from their core self, leaving them searching for wholeness.

One day when I was nine my brother's friend Ronnie dropped in. I liked seeing Ronnie because it was always playtime when he was around. I was in the kitchen, watching Mom prepare dinner when he arrived.

"Hello, Mrs. Hodge," Ronnie greeted my mother. "Is Jeff around?"

"No, Ronnie, he's over at Mike's house," Mom told him. Then he spotted me.

"Hey, Elaine, how are you today?"

"Good," I said, grateful that he'd even noticed me.

"Do you wanna go outside and shoot some basketball hoops?"

"Sure, that'd be great," I said, and we headed outside to play basketball.

A couple of days later, Ronnie came to visit again, and again Jeff was not at home. Mom was busy fixing dinner and watching over my younger brother and sister. Instead of leaving, Ronnie turned to me and said, "Elaine, do you want to go down to the basement and roller skate?" "Yeah, let's go," I replied, remembering the pleasure of past events. I loved to roller skate. My brothers and sisters and I spent many hours downstairs skating. Often, Ronnie joined us.

As we walked down the old, wooden stairs to the basement, a musty odor greeted us. I inhaled deeply, welcoming the smell, for it brought back fond memories of me helping Mom with the laundry. When I was four, she had me sit high on the steps, reach my little hands through the railing, and hang the socks with clothespins on the end of the line. I felt like a big girl as I helped her with the laundry and was so pleased to have some alone time with her. Getting any one-on-one time with Mom was rare.

The basement was always cool and damp, with spider webs dangling from the corners. There were two adjoining rooms, one for the washer, dryer and furnace and the other for the car. The floor was concrete and there was a doorway at each end of the two rooms, so we could skate around in a circle. A single light bulb hung from the ceiling, lighting the basement. One evening my brother Greg had decided to throw a tee shirt over the light to cut down on the glare and give the basement an eerie feeling. It was fun skating in the dimly lit basement until *poof*, the shirt went up in flames, starting a fire. Greg and the boys quickly threw some water on it and put it out.

But in the basement this day Ronnie started acting strangely. Instead of putting on his skates, he just stared at me with probing eyes. *What's going on?* He walked over, gave me a hug, and pulled up my tee shirt. I stepped back and asked, "What are you doing?" He smiled and said, "It's okay, I just want to look at you." I was afraid but didn't know what to do. He undressed me and then stood gawking at my naked body. I began shaking, the cool air and Ronnie's behavior sending shivers up my spine. Feeling totally embarrassed, I tried to cover my naked body with my hands, but Ronnie moved them away. He told me I was pretty and to put my clothes back on. Then he said, "This is our little secret. Don't tell anyone." I nodded my head yes while feeling totally confused.

After we came upstairs, Mom invited Ronnie to stay for supper. I was uncomfortable sitting at the table with him after what had just happened. I ate quickly, said, "I have to go to my room and finish my homework," and left.

Ronnie came over again in a few days, and I noticed that he kept showing up when Jeff wasn't home. I wondered if anyone else was aware of that. Mom always seemed too busy cleaning, cooking, or watching the babies to pay much attention.

Ronnie took my hand and led me to the basement to skate. Once there, he removed my top, unzipped his pants, and pulled out his thing. I was so afraid. I had seen my younger brother's private part when he scampered out of the bathroom naked after a bath, but Ronnie's was bigger and harder. My heart raced and I wanted to run upstairs. *What if somebody comes downstairs and sees us?*

He told me to touch his private part. I shook my head no and said, "I don't want to." He took my hand and put it on his thing. The skin felt soft and weird. Then he said, "Why don't you kiss it?" as he pushed my head down toward it. I kissed it, feeling an indescribably icky uneasiness in the pit of my stomach. He put it in my mouth and told me to suck it. After a short time, he pulled it out and I saw a clear liquid coming out the end of it and thought it was crying. He put it back in my mouth and then suddenly jerked it out, and this white, sticky stuff squirted out all over my chest, dribbling down onto my shorts, as he let out a strange sound. I didn't know what he was doing, but it didn't feel right and I didn't like it. (To this day, I still have flashbacks to Ronnie and feel sick to my stomach whenever I see vanilla yogurt.)

He took a big red hankie out of his pocket, rubbed the mess off my chest and shorts, and said, "Get dressed." He was finished. I felt dirty. My polka dot top clung to my sticky chest and a strange odor was on my body. As soon as he left, I ripped off my shorts and top and buried them deep inside the clothes hamper, hoping Mom wouldn't notice the smell. I sat in the tub and scrubbed and scrubbed and scrubbed, trying to get the filth off my body. Finally, I could tell I was clean on the outside, but there was no soap that could erase the dirt I felt on the inside.

Over the next couple of years, Ronnie kept coming around. Sometimes Jeff would be home and sometimes he wouldn't. I was happy when Jeff was there because Ronnie would hang out with him and leave me alone. When Jeff was gone, I'd hear Ronnie's knock on the door and my whole body would tense up. I knew what was coming. I was trapped. I didn't know what to do. I couldn't stop it. I felt ashamed but too afraid to go against him. He'd take me down the creaky basement steps, pull down my pants, and rub his thing up and down on my private part or stick it in my mouth, while I went away, floating above my body, my head in the clouds, waiting for it to end.

What I know now as a psychologist is that I was dissociating, mentally splitting off, leaving my body to survive the ordeal. Dissociation is a common defense mechanism in children who are abused and can be observed through their fantasy play, imaginary friends, or a deep trance-like state in which they appear vacant or dreamy. One of the chief features of dissociation is memory loss, and that is why many children who are sexually abused forget about their early trauma. As a therapist, I've encountered many women who have a 'sense' of being sexually abused as a child but can't come up with any specific memories.

As an adult, I knew I had been sexually abused by Ronnie even though I was out of my body and not present for most of the abuse; but for many years I had only sketchy memories of my father's abuse. It wasn't until I was in my forties that I began to have clearer recall of the details because I had dissociated at the time. So I clearly understand why some of my clients have no or limited recall surrounding their childhood abuse.

One summer, Ronnie went away for a couple of months to visit his grandparents. I was so happy that he was gone. I didn't have to be afraid or put up with his dirty stuff. I wanted it to be over and I never wanted to see him again. But one day in early August, as I was sitting in the front yard, his car pulled up. My insides churned and I wanted to throw up. I looked at him and thought, *No matter what I have to do, he's not going to touch me again. I can't stand it. I don't like it! I've never liked it. No more.*

I was only eleven years old and he was seventeen. My heart pounded so hard in my chest I was sure he saw it through my shirt. When he said, "Hey, Elaine, let's go downstairs and skate," I lied and said, "I don't feel good and don't want to play today." His face dropped. He got the message. Ronnie left and quit bothering me and I felt so relieved and proud of myself for standing up to him.

Sadly, this was not the last time I would experience sexual abuse. One day my girlfriend Judy and I were riding our bikes around the local high school. Judy and I hung out together all the time and she was my salvation – the cool breeze in the midst of my sweltering home life. On this particular day, we spotted a man sitting in a dark-blue car with his window down. He waved and called, "Come here, girls." Innocently, we rode over to the car to see what he wanted. He abruptly opened the car door and sat there stark naked from the waist down. Shocked by the sight of his penis, we both screeched and pedaled away as fast as we could.

When we felt safe, we stopped to catch our breath and giggled nervously. We couldn't believe what had happened. Should we tell our moms? We didn't know what to do, but decided not to say anything. I was always afraid of being blamed.

My only escape from my alcoholic home and sexual abuse was school and church. I loved going to school and church and being around the nuns and priests. They were my models. They loved God and had chosen to serve Him, and I wished to do the same. As a child, I gobbled up all the books I could find on the lives of the saints, those I wished to emulate: St. Theresa the Little Flower, St. John of the Cross, St. Teresa of Avila, St. Joan of Arc – my heroes. I even took the confirmation name Theresa in honor of the Little Flower.

I joined the Sodality, a lay church organization dedicated to increasing piety, devotion, and love of God. We met weekly with our parish priest to study religious literature and say our rosary. We were encouraged to go to Mass and Communion every day, which I faithfully did. I liked being around other young people who were serious about their faith and practiced it fervently.

The Sodality also engaged in 'spiritual works of mercy', admonishing sinners by pointing out their errant ways. One of our 'works of mercy' involved Father driving us to the lookout in Devou Park, the local lovers' lane, where we walked around shining our flashlights on parked cars to discourage teenagers from committing sins of the flesh. At the time, we thought we were doing such a worthy deed, but looking back I can't believe I actually did this and didn't get shot.

Because of my deep religious fervor, I was chosen, along with another girl, to go to the bishop's house once a week to recite the rosary on the radio. The bishop would say the first half of the prayer and we would respond with the second half. Afterward, the bishop would give us his blessing after we had knelt and kissed his gigantic ruby-stoned ring, and then hand us a holy card or some other religious item.

In the eighth grade, my teacher and school principal, Sister Rose, chose me to be part of the annual church ceremony of the crowning of Mother Mary. Reverently, I carried Mary's crown on a satin pillow in a procession through the church as the other children sang devotional hymns. I felt so honored to be selected for this role, for I had a deep devotion to Mother Mary. When we arrived at her statue, another classmate took the crown off the pillow and placed it on Mary's head.

All the recognition that the nuns bestowed on me through my grade-school years made me feel important and elevated my battered and bruised ego.

There are the good guys and bad guys, the cops and robbers, the saints and sinners, the abused and the abusers. I was one of the good guys abused by the bad guys until the summer of my twelfth year, when things changed. I babysat our neighbor's two children, a boy two years old and a girl who was three. While changing the boy's diaper, I became curious, looked at his penis, and without thinking, touched it. Immediately, I felt guilty. *I did something wrong. Why did I do it?* I thought about my dad and Ronnie touching me and how horrible I felt. How could I have done the same thing? Now I had more guilt to stuff into my overloaded backpack that was already weighing me down.

Not until years later did I realize it was not the same. I was twelve years old, not even starting to develop. There's a difference between a child's curiosity and a grown adult abusing a child. But I didn't know this at the time and felt deeply ashamed. I also didn't know that children who are sexually abused have a greater tendency to become hypersexual, either through excessive masturbation, sexual acts upon younger children, or adolescent promiscuity.

That marked the end of my babysitting career, for I never got invited back. I worried over the unknown. *Did he tell his mom? Did she know? Was she going to tell my mother?* I sweated for a few weeks until I realized my secret was safe. Mom wasn't going to find out, but I knew, and my deed haunted me for many years.

4

Catholic High School

It was the first day of classes in my sophomore year at the all-girls Catholic high school I attended. The two-story concrete school was adjacent to a large Victorian mansion that housed the nuns, our teachers. The two buildings were connected by a covered walkway, making it easy to pass back and forth.

All of us girls sat quietly at our desks waiting for our French teacher to arrive.

Dressed like a room full of identical twins, we were wearing pleated plaid skirts that reached down to our calves, white blouses, green blazers, and black-and-white saddle shoes. Our uniforms modestly covered our bodies. As good Catholic girls, we were admonished not to wear red clothes (the devil's color), patent leather shoes (they reflect up) or any tight clothing when away from school. Today red is my favorite color, for Native Americans believe it is the color that calls in the good spirits rather than the bad.

When I wasn't in school, I followed the good nuns' advice and didn't wear tight sweaters or short skirts and usually dressed in jeans and a flannel shirt. I had a nice figure and liked my body, but I didn't want to be seen as a sex symbol, and I certainly didn't want guys pursuing me for sex. That had been the story of my childhood: my father and Ronnie using and abusing me as a sexual object. I was desperate for it to end.

My thoughts drifted back to last year when I had a traumatic experience with my dentist, a man in his forties who wore a white coat and small white mask over his nose and mouth, looking like an alien ready to invade my body. I detested going to the dentist. The odor of novocaine and mercury permeated the sterile office, and the sound of the drill sent shivers through my entire body.

The drilling went on and on until I felt it would reach my toes. Often, it was so painful I wanted to cry.

On this visit, my dentist strategically placed his instruments on my chest and, when he reached for one, he took a feel of my breast. At first, I felt confused and not clear about what was happening. *Am I imagining things? Is my barometer off-kilter here because of my early abuse?* I doubted my own judgment about whether a man's behavior was appropriate or not, and even if it were blatantly inappropriate I had a hard time speaking up. Then a girlfriend told me my dentist had done the same to her. Then I knew!

The bell rang and in walked my French teacher, Sister Mary Victoria. I was dumbstruck. She was so beautiful. Even though she wore a black habit extending down to her old lady style black shoes, draped with a scapular and crucifix and with a veil on her head, I could still see her beauty. A snippet of coal-black hair above her forehead jutted out from under her veil. Her skin was silky white and her eyes were steel blue. She was young and vivacious and I fell in love with her immediately.

Surprisingly, she showed a great deal of interest in me. I followed her around like the proverbial puppy dog, wanting to please her, and even skipped lunch to go to the nuns' chapel to pray, knowing she would be there. Every good Catholic girl thinks about becoming a nun, and I was no exception. I decided that I wanted to go into the convent and be just like Sister Mary Victoria.

'Vic', the nickname the students gave her, became my confidante. I looked forward to meeting with her after school and telling her about my father's drinking and how it hurt me. She listened and understood. For the first time in my life I had found someone to talk to and, like a camel finding water in the desert, my emotional drought was quenched. Most days I stayed after school and talked to Vic, which disturbed my mother, who thought I might be revealing too much about our family. But I needed someone to listen to me, and I talked for hours to Vic about everything except the sexual abuse. That was one deep dark secret I couldn't share with anyone. I felt too ashamed.

I did tell her I masturbated, something I felt terribly ashamed of because the Church taught that it was a mortal sin. But the only way I could escape the craziness at home was to get lost in pleasuring myself, which temporarily blocked out the pain. Vic told me I had to stop and gave me a relic of St. Maria Goretti, a young martyr who died from multiple stab wounds inflicted by her rapist after she refused him because of her love for Jesus. Sister said, "Pin it to your underwear and it will help." It did for a couple of weeks, until one night the fighting became unbearable. I masturbated.

The next morning I went to Vic's desk, placed the relic on the corner, and returned to my seat. I hung my head, knowing she understood what this meant. It hurt so much to disappoint her. Later that day, Sister gave the relic back and said, "Keep trying." I was relieved. *She still liked me.*

Throughout my sophomore year we continued exchanging the relic, and I kept going to Confession. I couldn't seem to help myself. My self-esteem had already been in the gutter, but with all the masturbating, it slipped into the sewer. I was such a bad person, a sinner. I didn't know then that compulsive sexual behavior is one of the symptoms of childhood sexual abuse. Sex, food, alcohol and drugs are common compulsive behaviors that sexual abuse victims use to cover the pain, anger and depression that come from abuse.

During this same year, a young priest from the local parish came to our school once a week to teach a religion class. From the start, none of us girls liked him. He gave us the creeps. During class, he came to our desks, checked our assignments, and got all 'touchy-feely' by putting his hands on our shoulders or backs, something a priest was not supposed to do. Then he would lecture us on modesty of dress while trying to look up our skirts, saying, "Girls, you need to always keep your legs together because boys want to look up your dress." Often he'd lace his lectures with inappropriate sexual comments as our faces blushed with embarrassment.

We told Vic what was going on, and she said she'd be in the office with the two-way speaker on to listen to what he said during our next class. When he arrived in class the following week, we sat waiting for the dirty talk to begin. Ten minutes into class the office phone rang, sounding loudly through our room speaker. As we sat in pretended ignorance, he gave us a mean look. He knew what was going on. Our clandestine efforts to get him removed from our classroom had failed, but they hadn't been completely in vain. He stopped his touching and obscene talk.

Another priest, Father Jorgen, came to the public swimming pool in our neighborhood and played games in the water with my girlfriend Judy and me. At first it was strange seeing him half naked in a bathing suit, but after we got over the initial shock, we had fun playing: throwing the ball, splashing each other, and racing. But then things got weird, as he told us to spread our legs so he could swim between them. It felt dirty, like we were doing something wrong. When he started water wrestling and...oops, *accidently* touched my breast, I knew he was up to no good. We began avoiding him.

It was extremely upsetting for me to see a priest act this way. I couldn't wrap my head around it because I had been taught that a priest is God's representative and can do no wrong. But I knew what Father was doing was wrong; he was a wolf in priest's clothing and his behavior sickened me.

All my disturbing sexual experiences with men – Father Jorgen, the priest at school, the dentist, my dad, Ronnie, and the stranger in the car – had left a residue of distrust. I didn't like men. In my mind, they were all alike; all they wanted was sex. I didn't respect them, and I had no need for them.

Throughout high school I didn't have much contact with boys, as they went to a separate Catholic high school across town. We saw little of each other except at the Saturday night Catholic Youth Organization dance. The church didn't want us to date or, heaven forbid, marry a non-Catholic, so it sponsored Catholic dances. Occasionally, a Protestant sneaked in, and one night the chaperones discovered there was a non-Catholic boy at the dance.

As Elvis Presley's lyrics to 'You Ain't Nothin' but a Hound Dog' blared through the loudspeakers, the chaperones chased the teenager through the auditorium, bumping into the dancers. The terrified boy leaped out the second-floor window to get away and crashed on the concrete below, breaking his leg. My heart wept as I watched him lay on the sidewalk, writhing in pain. *Something is wrong here. This happened just because he's a Protestant.* I thought about my girlfriend Marilyn, who lived up the street. I liked her a lot, but I had to sneak out to see her because my mother didn't want me playing with a Protestant. None of this made sense to me.

The Saturday after the boy broke his leg, I met my first boyfriend, Peter, at the dance. My heart went into overdrive when he asked if I wanted to dance. I swallowed hard and squeaked out a yes. He was the first guy who had paid attention to me, and he was oh-so good looking. He was also a good dancer, and we tore up the dance floor rocking and rolling, everyone watching as we put on a great show. One night he asked, "Do you want to go to my junior prom?" I wanted to scream "Yes, Yes, Yes" and jump into his arms. Instead, I acted cool and merely replied, "Sure."

Mom was happy for me and bought me a beautiful pink formal dress, which made me look and feel like a princess, all pretty and grown-up. Peter arrived at the front door looking handsome in his tux and carrying a white carnation corsage for me. Nervously, he pinned it on as Mom took pictures. She made sure Dad stayed hidden upstairs when Peter arrived, and I was grateful for that. I told Mom goodbye and we left in his shiny white Chevy Impala.

We drove to a fancy restaurant where Peter had reservations. The maitre d' showed us to our table, and we sat staring at each other as if we were perfect strangers, which really we were. We had never talked much; all we ever did was dance. So the conversation was stilted as we sat trying to act like adults in teenage bodies. The dinner was delicious, but I was uncomfortable with the conversation and felt relieved when we left.

At the prom, Peter twirled me around all evening on the dance floor as the priests and nuns mixed in, making sure we didn't stand too close when the occasional slow dance came on. I had a great time, and all and all it was a fun and innocent evening. Mom didn't allow me to date much after the prom, but that was all right with me because I really had my sights set on entering the convent.

The senior year is supposed to be the best year of high school, but for me it was the worst. My homeroom teacher, Sister James Marie, a recent transplant from the Northeast, felt God had punished her by sending her to teach uncouth Kentucky hillbillies. She referred to us as 'river rats' because the Ohio River was near our school. For some unknown reason, she took a special disliking to me. Although I was elected class president, she never allowed me to hold any meetings, and every time she got a chance she put me down.

One Monday she came to class and said, "Everyone who plans on going to college stand up." Since we were all in the college prep class, everyone stood up. She looked at me with disgust and said, "Hodge, sit down. You're too dumb to go to college." I flashed back to memories of my father calling all of us 'stupid' while we were growing up. I *felt* dumb. I slunk into my chair, totally humiliated, as my classmates let out nervous giggles.

I detested her, and one day I jumped at my chance to get revenge. As she was complaining about our manners and calling us 'trashy', she said, "I wish I could take a slow boat to China to get away from you girls." That did it. I had had enough. I piped up and said, "Well, I'll buy you a one-way ticket." The class erupted in laughter, but that remark sealed my fate. I had committed the unforgivable crime of smarting off to a nun. After that, she made my life hell and tried to get me kicked out of school. Vic told me to be on my best behavior so I could finish my senior year, which I did.

Even though Sister James Marie put a damper on my last year, she did not squelch my desire to enter the convent. In my mind, one bad apple doesn't ruin the tree, so I proceeded with my plans to become a nun. Even though I greatly admired Vic, I wanted to go to a different convent – not a teaching order but one where the nuns worked with troubled girls, like the Good Shepherds. I figured all my difficult experiences would help me understand these girls. I applied to the Good Shepherds and was summoned to an interview with the head nun of the novitiates.

We met in a small, austere parlor with a couple of dark wooden chairs, an end table, and a lamp, a reflection of the convent's simplicity of religious life. I wore a long, modest dress that reached to my calves. Sister was rather cold and serious, and I felt uncomfortable. I fought my nervousness and explained why I was interested in their order and why I wanted to become a nun. I spoke about my lifelong desire to serve God and help others.

What I didn't say, and didn't know at the time, was that I also needed to find a safe refuge away from abusive men. The convent would be the perfect solution. When my older sister was seventeen, she dreamed of marrying her boyfriend, having children, and living a happy life. When I was seventeen, I wanted to do everything I could to avoid men and sex.

Sister told me she would consider my application and dismissed me. A couple of weeks later, I received a brief letter merely stating that my application had been denied. There was no explanation. The rejection tore me apart. I had lost my dream, and I slipped into despair. Negative thoughts swirled through my head: *Something's wrong with me. I'm not good enough. God doesn't want me. I'm a sinner. Maybe she thinks I'm more troubled than the girls they're trying to help.* My heart ached. What was I going to do? Depressed and lost, I decided to go to work after graduating.

5

Going to Work

I began working for the IRS processing tax returns. Amazed at my luck in landing a government job with good pay, I realized I could now buy all the things I wanted. I started spending my money like a drunken sailor, purchasing a car, golf clubs, and a diamond watch for my mother – remembering those delicious cherry pies she baked for me.

My boss, an overweight, middle-aged black woman, sat at her desk polishing her nails, reading magazines, and chatting on the phone, while we labored away like work horses. The woman next to me said, "Our boss is tenured, which means she can't be fired, so she doesn't do any work." *How does she get by with that?* I wondered. This was my first experience with the ineffective policies of government. It boggled my mind and didn't seem fair, but like a turtle retreating into a shell, I put my head down and went back to work. As a bright-eyed seventeen-year-old, I was glad to have a job; and if I stayed long enough, I might become tenured.

The tax work was monotonous and boring, sending my brain into a mental stupor. I dreaded going to work and hungered for more intellectual stimulation. My chance came when a private secretarial position opened up with another government agency. The job would be more demanding and was an increase in pay and status.

On the day of the interview I wanted to look my best, so I put on a fancy beige dress, high heels, and extra makeup and coifed my hair. I tried to look older than my seventeen years, thinking the boss would be looking for a mature woman. With hands shaking and internal jitters, I went to meet him. He immediately put me at ease by saying he was a fellow Catholic. We had a connection. I relaxed and took a deep breath. He talked about his wife and three sons and mentioned that one son was attending Notre Dame University. The more he talked, the more I liked him, and he must have liked me because he hired me on the spot. I was elated. *Not bad for a little Kentucky 'river rat'.*

Tim, my new boss, was 52 years old and had an overpowering presence, standing six-foot-three, with a husky build, pure white hair, and a gruff voice. I liked his strength and maturity and believed I had been placed in good hands. He took me under his wing and treated me like the daughter he never had, while he became the good dad I never had. I looked to him as a father figure who could give me the guidance and attention I had never received from my own dad.

As I sat at my desk one day poring over a pile of folders, Tim approached me and asked, "How would you like to go to Notre Dame with me and my wife, meet my son, and watch a Fighting Irish football game?" I could hardly contain my joy as I replied, "That would be great." Secretly, I wondered, *Is he trying to set me up with his son? That's fine with me,* I thought. *Nothing like a rich, intelligent Notre Dame boy!*

The university campus was huge, with stately buildings, tree-lined walkways, two lakes, beautiful statues, and the famous golden dome sitting atop the main building. The campus was gorgeous and so was Tim's son, but unfortunately there was no chemistry between us.

In the afternoon we went to the football game between arch rivals Notre Dame and Penn State. As we entered the stadium the roar of the crowd generated an electrifying energy. There's nothing like a Notre Dame football game to get the juices flowing! We screamed and cheered for every play, joining in the school spirit. Notre Dame squeaked out an exciting 21 to 20 win.

After the game, Tim, his wife, his son, and I headed out to dinner at an Italian restaurant, where Tim picked up the tab. It was a great weekend and I enjoyed being with Tim and his family. My family gatherings were often chaotic and stressful, so it was nice to be around a stable and fun-loving family.

Tim invited me to other family gatherings, took me to lunch at expensive restaurants, bought me gifts, and treated me like a princess. Undoubtedly, Lady Luck had taken me by the hand. But as I soon found out, everything comes with a price tag. Tim began leaving little notes on my desk. At first, he complimented me on my good work. Then he told me how much I meant to him, and eventually he said he was falling in love with me. I was flattered and wanted him to like me, but not in this way. He had a wife, and to me he was like a father, not a lover. I wasn't even attracted to him.

The notes continued but took on an increasingly disturbing slant, saying things he'd like to do to me sexually. I was dumbfounded but didn't know what to do. It became his little game, slipping notes and fantasizing. I didn't like it, but I couldn't seem to go against him. I didn't want to lose my job. The tightness in my chest returned, along with tears. It was all so familiar. Once more I was being pulled into the dark world of sexual secrets and powerlessness.

The secretary in the nearby department kept a watchful eye as Tim passed his notes. I'm sure she knew something was going on, and every time he handed me a note, my face blushed with embarrassment. I told myself they were only words, not actions, and I could ignore them. Shortly, however, things got worse.

One day at lunch time, Tim said to me, "I have to go to the bank vault and need you to come along and help with some recordkeeping." Happily – and naively – I obliged. He hailed a cab and we rode to the bank. The bank manager, who obviously knew Tim, shook his hand and gave him a friendly greeting, and they exchanged a few words. He then handed Tim a key to the bank vault and the two of us descended a dimly lit stairway to the basement. Tim unlocked the heavy steel vault door and pushed it open, the wheels screeching along the concrete floor.

Inside was a bare nine by twelve-foot room with a small metal table in the center. The walls were lined with locked vaults chiseled into the concrete where customers could place their valuables.

I jumped as Tim slammed the door, shut and locked it. I was trapped inside with him. A sly grin came over his face and he said, "Go over to the corner, take off your underpants, crouch down, lift your dress, and spread your legs so I can look at you."

I flashed back to a similar sexual scene in the basement with Ronnie. My shoulders tensed and fear surged through my body. *It's happening again. I'm frightened. Is he some kind of sex pervert? A voyeur?* His demanding voice interrupted my thoughts. "Do as I say."

My stomach churned and I thought I might vomit as I took off my underwear, squatted down, lifted my dress, and spread my legs, providing Tim with a free peep show. I was so embarrassed and disgusted with myself. *Why am I going along with this?* Today, I see how the early abuse by my father and Ronnie stripped me of the rights to my body and taught me to do what men wanted sexually. I didn't know how to say no. I was powerless. I didn't even know I had a choice. I detested my father and Ronnie for abusing me and setting me up for this degrading behavior. It felt so dirty and wrong. My heart wept silent tears for that little girl, and now the adult woman, who was suffering such indignities.

The obscene notes and visits to the bank continued, and each time we walked down the bank staircase and I heard Tim's rubber soles behind me squeaking against the concrete steps, I wanted to disappear. As he closed the heavy door, my breathing became shallow and my body froze up with dread. I knew what was coming.

Around this same time, I befriended a middle-aged woman named Diane at work.

As we were having an intimate woman-to-woman talk, I told her I was still a virgin. So far, Tim's sexual behavior had consisted of obscene notes and voyeurism at the bank, but no touching. Diane acted surprised and said, "Elaine, it's about time you experienced sex." Although she didn't mean to, Diane left me feeling as if something was wrong with me. She didn't know I was raised a strict Catholic and that good Catholic girls don't engage in sex until they're married. She also didn't know I had been sexually abused and tended to avoid men and intimacy.

But here we were in the 1960s at the beginning of the hippie and sexual liberation movement, where traditional sexual values were being discarded along with other outdated cultural mores. It was a different time with different energy, and people were having sex outside of marriage with multiple partners while I was still imprisoned by my narrow Catholic beliefs. I thought, *Maybe she's right. I need to break free, let go of my rigid values, forget about the past abuse, and experience sex. It has to happen sometime. Why not now and get it over with?*

Diane interrupted my thoughts. "I have a younger brother, Dan, who is thirty-five. You could be sexual with him." To me, the idea of having sex was like a chore, a task I had to complete to move into adulthood, similar to a sorority hazing. It had nothing to do with love, romance, or even sexual pleasure. It was just a step I had to take. Diane arranged for me to visit Dan at his nearby apartment at lunchtime. I told her I would be hungry, and she said Dan would get me a cheeseburger from McDonald's.

Nervously, I knocked on Dan's door. He quickly opened it and said hello. He seemed like a nice enough man, but I had no attraction to him. Dan handed me my cheeseburger and I sat on the couch munching it, more interested in the food than the sex. He asked if I was ready and I nodded yes. I had to get back to work. Dan slipped a condom on his erect penis, laid me down on the couch, slipped off my underpants, spread my legs, penetrated me, and ejaculated. 1...2...3...4...5. It was over so quickly that I was still chewing on my last bite of burger. The whole experience turned me off. It was so mechanical and uninteresting that I wondered what all the hype was about. If this was all there was to sex, forget it. I wanted nothing to do with it.

Meanwhile, back at work, Tim continued passing me his obscene notes and arranging for 'peek and see' visits at the bank vault. Soon his behavior escalated, with demands for a secret rendezvous at the local drive-in theater. I tried putting him off, knowing it was a bad idea, but he kept insisting, and finally I gave in, finding it hard once again to say no.

I drove my own car, he drove his, and when it was dark, I slipped out of my car and into his. Immediately, he started fingering me and touching my breast until he got aroused. Then he had me masturbate him until he came into his hankie. All the sexual play was about *his* pleasure and not mine. It was over pretty quickly, and I drove home to my parents' house, tears running down my cheeks, feeling empty and dirty. The reality was setting in. Tim didn't *love* me! He was just one more man using me as a sexual plaything. It had to stop. It was time to move on. I quit my job and started college full time.

I was so relieved to be away from Tim and happy to be attending college. I decided to major in psychology as a way to understand my father and his bizarre behavior. At the time, I didn't comprehend that my father was an alcoholic and that his disease was creating all the havoc in our home. In my mind, there was just something wrong with Dad and I wanted to know what it was. Dating didn't interest me at this time in my life, for men had just been trouble with a capital T. So, like a horse with blinders on, I focused on my goal, took an accelerated path of full loads all year, including summers, and graduated in two-and-a-half years.

I also chose to major in psychology so I could become a counselor and realize my dream of serving God by helping others. Even though I hadn't been accepted into the convent, I could still be of service to mankind. During college, I served as a Big Sister to a thirteen-year-old girl with an absentee mother, and traveled on weekends to the poverty-stricken Appalachian mountains of Kentucky to work with Father Beiting's Christian Appalachian Project. Rockcastle County, where Father Beiting was located, was one of the poorest counties in the country. Together with other college students, I worked in Father's thrift store and took groceries, supplies, and clothing to families living in dilapidated shacks nestled in the mountain hollows.

The contrast between the splendor of the majestic mountains and the squalor of these homes was overwhelming. It reminded me of the lyrics of the Kingston Trio's song 'Poverty Hill': "The summer folks call it Paradise Mountain but we call it Poverty Hill." It was gratifying for me to be able to alleviate the poverty of these mountain people in some small manner.

After graduating from college with a degree in psychology, I accepted a vocational counseling job with the State of Ohio. I was assigned to a sleepy little burg in the middle of the boonies. My duties involved outreach work: traveling around the rural community visiting young people and talking to them about jobs and vocational training. I was on my own. There was no office, and my days were spent working in the field.

I rented a room from a small gray-haired widow who ignored me and made it perfectly clear she wasn't interested in companionship but only needed the rent money. Not knowing anyone in town and living in an unfriendly environment, away from home and friends for the first time, I felt incredibly lonely.

Occasionally, my boss, Bob, came to check up on my work. He was responsible for the entire southern half of Ohio, so he only got to our town about every six to eight weeks. Bob was a lanky six-foot-three middle-aged man with dark brown hair and a dull personality. I didn't particularly like him, but I was isolated and hungry for companionship so I looked forward to his occasional visits. At least he was someone to talk to. Although at first he behaved in a professional manner, he had shifty eyes, which left me feeling uncomfortable; but he *was* my boss, so I acted friendly to stay on his good side.

Whenever Bob came to town we'd drive along the straight roads and farm fields to visit my clients. One day, he pulled off the main highway onto a remote dirt road and stopped at an isolated spot under a large oak tree. He said he wanted to talk about my cases, so I didn't think that anything about our stop was unusual. It was a beautiful, warm Indian summer day, the leaves on the oak tree sporting a brilliant shade of red after an early frost. The ground under the tree was coated with a blanket of fresh-fallen acorns, winter food for the squirrels. I could hear the birds chirping in the tree as the afternoon sun poured through the front windshield of Bob's dark-green sedan. I snuggled into my soft leather seat, waiting for him to start talking about my cases.

Without warning, he reached over, grabbed my shoulders, and pulled me close to him. The file folders in my lap slid to the floor. When he started fondling my right breast, I knew I was in trouble. I pulled away, but he roughly jerked me back, grasping me tightly with his powerful arms. Defenseless and frightened, I slipped into my childhood coping mechanism of dissociation, floating out of my body and watching from afar as everything moved in slow motion. He pulled up my dress, ripped off my panties, unzipped his fly, pulled out his red, swollen penis, climbed on top of me, and raped me.

I lay there in shock, squashed by the dead weight of his body. The nauseating stench of his harsh breath and pungent cologne assaulted my nostrils as I struggled for breath beneath him. Waves of disgust and humiliation washed over me. As I had so many times in the past, I felt dirty and violated. Finally, he climbed off me, saying only, "Put your panties back on." As I did, I felt the slime between my legs. Suppressing the urge to vomit, I thought, *I'm glad we're in his car and not mine. I don't want any smells or reminders of this day.* My attacker's voice interrupted my thoughts. "If you want to keep your job, you better not tell anyone. And if you do, I'll just say it was consensual." *It wasn't consensual. You raped me!* my mind screamed.

I nodded as if I understood, but inside I was raging. I wanted to shoot the son of a bitch. I thought back to my first boss, Tim, and how he had abused me. Now this jerk! *How can these men get away with this? What the hell! Do I have a flashing neon sign on my forehead that says, 'Rape Me'? Maybe I should have tried to fight him off. Hit him, kicked him, screamed. Is it my fault?* I was always blaming myself for not standing up to men, but I felt helpless. Tears streaked my cheeks. I felt so defeated, so powerless, so sad, so brokenhearted. I sat quietly in the front seat as Bob straightened himself up and then headed down the road to a client's house, acting as if nothing had happened. I put on a 'happy face' while still fighting the urge to throw up all over his new car.

I didn't know then that women who are sexually assaulted as children are twice as likely to be raped as adults.[4] We are less skilled at self-protection and are more apt to find ourselves in abusive and dangerous situations. Unless we gain more understanding and learn how to take care of ourselves, we are vulnerable to adult victimization.

After Bob left town, I knew I had to get away from him. I couldn't stand to see him one more time after what had happened. I looked into a transfer within the state system that would be out of Bob's jurisdiction. There was an opening in an inner-city section of Cleveland. Although I knew it might be challenging to work in a poor black ghetto, my desire to serve kicked in. I applied and promptly received the transfer. Evidently no one else was fighting for the position. A month later I moved to Cleveland and never saw Bob again.

Part II

Relationships and Sexuality

It is not uncommon for victims of childhood abuse to get stuck in a cycle of abuse. This is known as repetition compulsion and it describes the pattern in which victims of trauma find themselves constantly reliving the abuse.[5]
Laura Berman, Ph.D.

6

Victimization

I have never been married, and my longest intimate relationship lasted for four years (off and on), which was an eternity for me. I have had trouble maintaining and enjoying a committed relationship. Most of my significant relationships were with alcoholic men who further victimized me. Trust issues, anxiety, sexual difficulties, low self-esteem, and an inability to set healthy boundaries accompanied all of my relationships. These are some of the common symptoms of adult survivors of childhood sexual abuse.

Once a victim, always a victim – at least that's how it seems to go with children who are sexually abused. When a child assumes guilt and blame for the abuse, she thinks she did something to cause it: she didn't tell anyone, she was told it was her fault, it felt good, she didn't say no. As a result, she develops poor self-esteem. She sees herself as a bad person who doesn't deserve to be loved, and this sets the wheels in motion for victimization in her adult relationships. Desperate to find love and feel okay about herself, she puts up with unacceptable behavior.

As I've mentioned, children who are sexually abused find themselves in dangerous or unhealthy situations as adults due to a lack of protective skills and low self-esteem. They are psychologically weakened and vulnerable to additional physical, emotional, or sexual abuse in their relationships. Abusers can sense a survivor's vulnerability and they take advantage of it. It might be the fear in the woman's eyes when he raises his voice, or the puppy-dog look on her face that says, 'Please love me. I'll do anything for you', or her willingness to accept verbal abuse, or her lack of personal boundaries. It's as if the woman emits a pheromone that signals to a predator that she is there for the taking. I believe I did this in most of my adult relationships.

I got into my first intimate and abusive relationship when I was twenty-three and working in the ghetto of Cleveland as a vocational counselor. I lived and worked in the inner city, and all my coworkers and 95 percent of my clients were black. Another counselor in the office, David, a nice-looking, friendly, former all-American football player, began paying special attention to me. We had worked together on a few cases and he began making daily visits to my desk. I enjoyed talking with him.

On one of these visits, David seemed nervous as he fidgeted in his chair, and I knew he was going to ask me out. Suddenly, he popped the big question. "Would you like to go out on a date sometime?" I had to smile as I said yes. We made plans to go out that Saturday.

When Saturday arrived, my heart pounded like a teenager on her first date as I pulled clothes off their hangers and tried on one outfit after another. I had to have the right look: attractive but not too sexy. Finally I settled on a simple black dress. With shaking hands I carefully put on my makeup and then nervously stood at the window watching for David to arrive. I'd had only a handful of teenage dates before meeting David, so dating was still rather new to me.

David arrived looking very handsome in a pair of black dress pants and a white shirt. His eyes gave me an approving once-over and he said, "You look nice. Are you ready?" I nodded and he drove us downtown to a fancy white nightclub. As we walked in, people stared, but David and I ignored them, caught up in the magic of our first date. We dined, danced, talked, and laughed, having a great time.

Afterward, we drove back to my apartment and sat in the car talking, neither of us wanting to end the date. David put his arm around me, pulled me close, and gave me a tender kiss. It felt sweet. He continued kissing me as his hand wandered to my breast. My shoulders tightened and I pulled away saying, "Stop,

I don't want to go any further and risk getting pregnant." I really didn't plan on having sex on our first date. David assured me that I wouldn't get pregnant and that it was okay. *Did he have a vasectomy?* I didn't know. He kept assuring me that I wouldn't get pregnant as he continued kissing and fondling me. The ball was rolling and I couldn't stop it, even though I knew there was a risk of my getting pregnant. I remembered my dad's advice: "If you want to be happy, give men what they want." I knew what David wanted – sex.

I was torn. I liked David and didn't want to lose him, so I gave in to the sex, thinking that would bring me love. The message in my head from my early sexual abuse was that who I was wasn't good enough – that my real value was as a sexual object – and that message continued to filter into my adult relationships. Looking back, it grieves me to see how I lost so much of myself by letting those old messages run my life.

Not only did my alcoholic father sexually abuse me, he verbally abused me as well. According to him, I was stupid, lazy, and no good. 'Stupid' was his favorite word, and he called me stupid repeatedly. I recall how he criticized me years later when I told him I was receiving my doctoral degree in psychology. Instead of complimenting me on my achievement, as I thought he would, his acid tongue spit out, "Oh great, now you'll be so goddamn smart no man will want you." I felt as though he'd ripped my chest open, pulled my heart out, and stomped on it. How could a father be so mean? His cruel words cut to the core of my being, attacking my intelligence and desirability. I thought, *No matter what I accomplish, I'll never be good enough.*

No wonder I was always searching for a man's approval and love to feel better about myself. And now I was doing it again with David. Our relationship began with me giving my power away while David called the shots. I was merely along for the ride, but little did I know how rough the ride would be.

David took over the relationship, dictating what we should

do, when and how. I was passive and subservient to him, qualities that go along with a victim mentality. Our days were filled with work and our nights with partying. David introduced me to pot, liquor, and wild sex. I'd like to say that I at least enjoyed the sex, but I didn't. My earlier sexual experiences had been abusive and forceful, and now that I was in a relationship where mutual pleasuring should have been possible, I couldn't stop the flashbacks and disturbing feelings. Oral sex repulsed me because it reminded me too much of Ronnie's abuse. But intercourse was no better, because afterward I'd have to take a shower to clean the mess off my body. I knew this wasn't normal, but I wasn't normal when it came to sex.

I tried to forget the past, but it kept showing up in the present, like a disturbing, repeated nightmare. I wanted to enjoy sex, so I started faking an orgasm, cooing "ooh" and "ah", waiting for my body to overtake my troubled mind. David didn't seem to notice that I couldn't relax, couldn't shut off my disturbing thoughts, or couldn't have an orgasm. He was too lost in his own pleasure.

One day David and I went to the dreaded Motor Vehicle Division to get a license plate for my car. Waiting in line at the MVD was a nightmare. For three long hours we stood in line. David was restless and so was I. I tried to pass the time by occasionally chatting with folks in front of and behind us in line. David was quiet and subdued.

Finally, we got the license and headed for home, exhausted and irritable. David was driving. Next thing I knew, I saw stars and then blackness as I faded into unconsciousness. As I came to, I heard David raging at me. "Don't you ever flirt with anyone again!" I didn't know what he was talking about, but my jaw ached and I realized he had hit me and knocked me out. Terrified, my whole body tightened up as he continued raging. I'd never seen him act this way, so out of control.

I sat frozen in panic, afraid to move or speak, tears streaming down my face, waiting for his anger to subside. All I could think about was how to get out of the moving car before he hit me again. He slowed down as we approached my apartment, and while the car was still rolling to a stop I leaped out and ran inside, locking the door behind me. David banged on the door. I ignored him, and he left.

David called repeatedly, leaving messages on my answering machine saying how sorry he was. I didn't return his calls but still had to see him at work. One day he came to my desk teary-eyed and told me he was so sorry. He appeared repentant, and I missed him. I was lonely. I gave in. I told him, "If it ever happens again, we're through for good." He nodded his head and said, "I'm sorry. It *won't* happen again." I believed him.

Today, I think of all the women I have counseled over the years who have been in physically abusive relationships. Usually I encourage them to get out of the relationship and find a safe place to live. I didn't take my own advice with David because I was so needy for his love and thought so little of myself. Eventually, I left Cleveland and the relationship ended.

My neediness led me to continue my search for a man who would make me whole. Going to the bars and looking for Mr. Right became my weekend routine. Come Saturday night I'd put on my good jeans, a nice sweater and cowboy boots, apply some makeup, fix my hair, and walk two blocks to the local bar. After a couple of drinks and chatting and dancing with a guy, if I thought he might be *the one*, I'd bring him home.

The next morning I'd wake up lying next to a stranger who smelled like a brewery and whose name I couldn't remember. *What did I see in this guy?* These 'one-night stands' left me feeling empty and depressed. Plus, I was engaging in reckless and dangerous behavior, which is not uncommon for a sexually abused child. I promised myself I would quit going to the bars, but then another Saturday night would arrive and my loneliness and neediness drove me out the door.

Then one Saturday evening a nice-looking man wearing dark-brown dress pants, an attractive sweater, and loafers sat down next to me. He stood out from the other men in the bar, who were all wearing jeans and sweatshirts. "Hi, I'm Chuck," he said, as he extended a hand to me. I shook his hand and looked him over, liking what I saw. He had light-brown hair, blue eyes, and a nice build. Chuck told me he was a CPA and financial advisor. It was easy to talk to him and we chatted the evening away talking about work, sports, and city politics. *How refreshing to talk to a guy about something other than hunting and the weather,* I thought.

During the evening, Chuck had one drink after another while I nursed my second gin and tonic. We talked till closing time and as we headed out the door together he asked, "Do you feel like coming over to my house?" "Sure," I replied, excited that he asked and feeling flattered. I knew we'd end up having sex, but in my mind that was okay because he was interesting and this could lead to a good relationship.

Nervously, I followed Chuck in my car down a winding road into the woods. I lit up a joint and took a couple of hits to calm myself down. When we arrived at his beautiful wood home nestled in the trees, I thought, *This guy is pretty well off!*

Once inside, Chuck fixed me a drink and we sat on the couch and started to make out. I felt a little lightheaded and realized I was pretty high from the dope I had smoked.

After the touching became hot and heavy, I excused myself and went to the bathroom. I had to put in my diaphragm. I stripped down to my underwear, and when I returned Chuck was sitting on the couch naked with an erection. As soon as I sat down, he pulled off my underpants, climbed on top of me, grabbed my hair, and jerked my head back. "Tell me you want me," he said. I thought, *What's going on here?* He continued pulling my hair hard, until it hurt, saying, "Tell me you want me to fuck you, tell me to give it to you, talk dirty."

I was scared and totally turned off. I'd had no idea this guy had violent sexual proclivities. Obviously, Chuck wanted to get off by subduing me and hearing filthy talk. I felt like I was being raped. My heart started racing and I was terrified, unsure of how violent he might become. Here I was alone in the woods with a crazy man. *Stay calm*, I told myself. *Go along with it and get out of here safely.* So I said, "Fuck me, I want you so much, give it to me. I want you. I want you. Fuck me. Fuck me." That did it. He had an orgasm, let go of my hair, and lay back on the couch exhausted.

I got up, went to the bathroom, and quickly threw on my clothes. I grabbed my purse and darted out of the bathroom toward the front door. Out of the corner of my eye, I saw Chuck still lying on the couch. Fearful that he might try to stop me, I bolted out the door, jumped in my car, and locked the door. My body was trembling and I felt paranoid because I was higher than usual. *Drive slowly and watch the road*, I repeated to myself. I had a long thirty-minute drive home, fighting to stay focused and keep my car under control. I berated myself for being high and putting myself in a risky situation. Maybe I missed the signs and didn't make a good judgment. There are weird people out there and Chuck was one of them. I needed to be careful.

Arriving home safely, I went to bed, where I spent a restless, fitful night, and woke up feeling sick to my stomach. The nightmarish evening had been so degrading – devaluing me as a woman and making me feel like a cheap prostitute. Negative and critical thoughts spun through my head. *Why did I put myself in that situation? I should have known better.* I didn't know then that I was throwing off vibes that marked me as a weak and vulnerable woman. Just being in the bar alone and picking up a stranger were sure signs of someone who was needy and didn't think very highly of herself. Chuck, like other abusers, merely took advantage of my vulnerability.

7

Unavailable Men

I want a girl, just like the girl who married dear old Dad.
Harry von Tilzer

It's no secret that many men marry women just like their mothers, while women marry men like their fathers. My pattern was getting involved in painful, dramatic relationships with abusive alcoholics like my father, going after the love I never received from him. If I could find a man similar to my father and have him fall in love with me, I could fix things from my childhood. I was recreating my childhood trauma and trying to change it. Of course, this never worked, because the alcoholics I dated were in love with the bottle and unable to give me the consistency, trust, and love I needed.

Reflecting back, I see how my chasing after alcoholics and hopeless relationships allowed me to avoid intimacy and commitment. I didn't trust men and was terrified of being hurt again so I became relationship avoidant. If I started to have deep feelings for a man, I would criticize him unmercifully, trying to drive him away. I would mentally test his trustworthiness, and when he failed the test, as unavailable men always do, I'd withdraw from the relationship.

The effects of childhood sexual abuse can show up in many ways, and one of them is in choosing relationships with unavailable men. A man might be unavailable because he is married, has an addiction, is unable to make a commitment, cheats, or is emotionally distant. Whatever the reason, he is not suitable material for a good partnership.

The most unavailable man I ever dated was an alcoholic gay priest. We worked closely together in the same department at a

Catholic college. I liked Ed immediately and we ended up spending a great deal of time together. I felt myself developing romantic feelings toward him, sensing all the while that he was having the same type of feelings for me. It appeared especially obvious when he invited me to travel to his home to meet his mother. She thought, of course, that we were just colleagues and friends, but a relationship was developing and soon we became sexual.

Ed drank a lot, and one night in bed he told me he was gay and confused by his feelings for me. His disclosure didn't really bother me because I figured I could get him to quit drinking and change his mind about being gay. The idea of getting a priest to fall in love with me was so enticing. Getting Ed to leave the priesthood, renounce his gay orientation, and marry me would be the solution to everything and prove how special I was. Of course, that didn't happen. I lived in the fantasy of how things *could* be rather than the reality of how they were.

Looking back, I can see how Ed was safe – the epitome of an unavailable man. Deep down, I knew I didn't have to worry about commitment, marriage, or even a lasting relationship. The partnership was doomed from the start, enabling me to dodge my fears of commitment and intimacy.

I started another relationship with an alcoholic when I was living in the Upper Peninsula of Michigan and teaching at Northern Michigan University. I lived in the woods, isolated on the shores of Lake Superior. Feeling rather lonely one evening, I ventured out to the Lakeside Inn, a rural bar one mile from my house. As I opened the door, my nostrils were assaulted by the stench of stale beer. *I don't know how long I can hang out in this joint,* I thought. Seated at the bar were six men who probably called this place home. They were drinking and joking with each other. As I entered, they all turned on cue to gawk at me, making me feel like a bug under a microscope. Hurriedly, I headed to a corner table, sat down, and buried my head in a menu. The bartender approached and I ordered a grilled cheese sandwich, and when I asked for a glass of water I got that raised-eyebrow 'Oh no, not another cheapskate nondrinker' look.

Soon one of the men from the bar bellied up to my table. He was wearing a long-sleeved white shirt, tie, and dark-brown slacks and looked different from the rest of the men, who were dressed in flannel shirts, raggedy jeans, and blaze-orange hunting hats.

"Hi," he said with a smile. "I'm Leo the Lion."

"Hello, Leo the Lion," I replied with a chuckle.

"I was wondering if such a lovely lady as you would care to join me for a game of pool after you eat."

Leo was slurring his words slightly and obviously had been drinking heavily, but he was funny and charming, as many alcoholics can be. Being hungry for companionship more than for food, I accepted his invitation.

After I finished my sandwich, I signaled to Leo at the bar. He came to the pool table, dropped some coins in the money slots, and racked the balls. I grabbed a cue stick and joined him. We shot three games of pool and made small talk.

"Where do you work?" he asked.

"Oh, I work at the University."

"What's your name?"

"Elaine."

I gave only my first name because I didn't want to open anything up.

He told me he worked at the local bank and we chatted back and forth and banged the balls around the table. I had fun. It was good to have some company, and I had to head home too soon.

Several days later I was surprised to receive a phone call from Leo at work. I was puzzled by how he'd found my phone number without a last name.

"Would you like to go out dancing this Saturday?" he asked. My head said no but my heart – and mouth – replied yes.

Saturday evening I met Leo at the Tioga Bar, which was down the road a mile from the Lakeside Inn. Bars were certainly not a scarcity in the Marquette area. The Tioga had a live band with country music. Leo was a great dancer and he swung me around the floor to the lively beat of 'Rocky Top'. When the 'Beer Barrel Polka' played, he grabbed me again, and we slow-danced to Tammy Wynette's 'Stand by Your Man'. I felt comfortable in his arms and wanted to be closer to him. Our bodies moved so well together while dancing I knew we'd be good lovers.

As the evening progressed, Leo kept pouring down the beer and feeling no pain. I sipped on a couple of gin and tonics and noticed how hammered he was getting. His drinking was no mystery; he didn't try to hide it or slow it down. It was clear he was an alcoholic, and I knew that to be with him I just had to accept that fact. He was easygoing and had a good sense of humor. Maybe I'd be able to overlook the drinking, I rationalized. As the evening wound down, he held me once again in his arms for another slow dance and whispered in my ear, "Would you like to come home with me?" I cooed back, "Yes."

My relationship with Leo helped fill some of the emptiness inside, for at last I'd found someone who cared about me. Leo adored me. His eyes lit up and a big smile crossed his face whenever he saw me. I loved him in return, putting up with his drinking, occasional impotency, and stinky beer breath, which reminded me of my father. I came full circle with Leo. When I was in bed with him, the familiar smell of alcohol on his breath created flashbacks to my father. Somehow, the two became intermingled. Unlike my father, however, Leo loved me and I loved him, and the lovemaking was mutual. At the time, I thought I had found what I was searching for.

I always knew where to find Leo in the evenings – at the Lakeside Inn. After he lost his job at the bank due to his drinking, he hung out at the bar all day long. It was baffling to see him sitting contentedly in a dingy, dark, and smelly bar all day when the sun was shining and Lake Superior was less than two hundred feet away. I'd sit next to him for a while, sipping on my Coke, and then become antsy and want to walk the beach. I'd invite him to come along, thinking he'd want to be with me, but he'd decline, saying he had to stay because Joe had bought him a drink.

Lined up in front of him like little toy soldiers were all these small white cups, purchased by cronies to provide free drinks. Continuing to buy for one another, they created an eternal procession of cups. What I didn't know at the time was that this is normal behavior for alcoholics. They want to drink, and surround themselves with buddies who will enable them. All the drinking began to bother me. I wanted to do more with my free time than sit in a bar. When I'd complain, Leo promised to cut back on his drinking.

One Thursday afternoon I went to my gynecologist for a yearly checkup. During the pelvic exam, a disturbing look appeared on the doctor's face, leaving me with an unsettling feeling. In a slow, halting voice he said, "There's a large growth on your uterus." I was shocked. As he continued on, reciting a list of possible causes, I heard only one word: *cancer.* Fear gripped my heart. I could hardly breathe. From a far-off place, I heard his cold, professional voice droning on. "If it's cancer, you have a slim chance of surviving." I left the office in a fog. Cars whizzed by, horns tooted, lights changed, but I was somewhere else, lost in my whirling thoughts. *Was I going to die?* Arriving home, I fell on my bed and sobbed. I was terrified.

Surgery was scheduled for the Friday of Easter weekend. My brother Randy flew in to be with me, and Leo would be there. The operation went smoothly, and I awoke Saturday morning to great news: no cancer. It was a large, nonmalignant ovarian cyst. I was ecstatic! Throughout the day, I drifted in and out of consciousness, still feeling the effects of the anesthetic. Finally, I told my brother and Leo to leave and get some rest. They were both exhausted. Randy was flying home the next day, but Leo promised to return first thing in the morning. I kissed them both goodbye and drifted off again into never-never land.

I awoke the next morning thinking about the Easter message of new life. I was so grateful to be alive. What a glorious day! I looked forward to Leo's arrival. The nurse helped me change into a fresh gown. I dabbed on a little makeup, combed my hair, and sat up in bed waiting for him. A couple of hours passed. I drifted off to sleep and woke up expecting Leo to be by my side. He wasn't. *Where is he? Maybe he slept in and is running late.*

A little dark-haired aide arrived with a liquid lunch. I wasn't hungry. Being sore and in pain, I asked for more medication. The afternoon dragged on and on. As the hours passed, I felt angry and hurt. *How dare he do this to me? Where is he? Could he be at the bar? No, not on Easter Sunday. It's probably closed, plus he promised to be here.*

The door swung open and I felt my heart skip a beat, but it was only the nurse coming to give me a shot. I didn't know which hurt worse, my stomach or my breaking heart. After dinner, the hospital chaplain stopped in, the only visitor of the day. Feeling sorry for myself, in pain, and upset with Leo, I began to sob. The priest was speechless and just patted my hand, trying to console me.

Early the next morning Leo burst into the room with a bouquet of flowers. That's the way it always was: he'd do something to upset me and then try to make up for it. I was furious and screamed, "Where have you been?" Averting my eyes and with a sheepish grin, he said, "I stopped at the bar to have *one* drink before heading to the hospital." He never left the bar.

At that moment, the harsh reality of addiction became real for me. Alcohol had raised its ugly head and won. Leo couldn't control his drinking. He'd promise to show up, cut back on his drinking, pick up more responsibility, love me forever – until that first drink touched his lips, and then it was over. He'd keep drinking as his promises evaporated like morning mist. Sadly, I told Leo to leave. It was over. I'd had enough of his drinking and I didn't want to be with a man who was undependable. I cried myself to sleep – again.

After Leo, I seemed to slip deeper and deeper into depression. I couldn't understand why my relationships weren't working and felt frustrated and defeated. When Brad, a married alcoholic, came into my life, I hit bottom.

I needed a building project done at my house, and my friend mentioned that her neighbor Brad, a carpenter, might want to do the work. I called him. He came to my house and I explained the project. Since he was out of work, he was more than eager to take on the job, so I hired him on the spot.

Brad was a ruggedly handsome outdoorsman with baby-blue eyes that a woman can imagine drowning in. At least this woman did. Each time his old pickup pulled into my driveway I felt like a teenager swooning over her first love. As my body responded, my mind swirled, conflicted by what I was feeling and the fact that he had a wife. My body won. Eventually, we slept together.

When it came to men, I had tunnel vision. Like my other boyfriends before Brad, it didn't make any difference whether the man was married, a priest, an alcoholic, an ax murderer, or all four. I wanted him to love me. My self-esteem was so low that I was desperate for a man's love and accepted whoever came along. Like a ball in a pinball machine, I bounced from one bad relationship to another. Brad was just one more.

Brad became my world. I catered to him when we were together and pined for him when we were apart. Every song reminded me of him, some making me smile and others bringing on tears. He would leave his wife soon – I knew it. He loved me. He'd be with me. One day he surprised me with a beautiful turquoise and coral ring. He had a matching one. He called it a commitment ring. Yes, we would be together soon.

Brad left his wife. He was finally mine, and I was so happy. I had dreamt of this day. He moved into a little cabin in the woods near my home. We spent a lot of time together doing the things I'd imagined: camping, fishing, hiking, and dancing. But something wasn't right. Brad became moody and irritable and drank more. He went to visit his home a couple of times a week, using his children as an excuse. After four months with me, suddenly, without warning, he moved back in with his wife. My world fell apart. I was devastated, convinced I couldn't live without him.

I swore it was over. Yet, the building project was not quite complete, so I allowed him to come back and finish it. Seeing him day after day weakened my resolve. I was so lonely.

Over the next two years, my life was a revolving door through which Brad swung in and out of my life. Being with him brought a high. Each time he returned to his wife I crashed and burned, reliving the nightmare of loss. But I held fast to the belief that one day we would be together for good.

One morning I answered the phone and was stunned to hear his wife's voice on the other end. She wanted to talk. Part of me wanted to hang up, but another part wondered what she had to say. I swallowed hard and agreed to talk. She told me that Brad had lied about everything. He hadn't left his house, she had kicked him out. He'd sleep with anyone who put up with his antics, drinking, and mood swings. He had used me. He didn't love me. There was no commitment and never had been.

I hung up the phone, jerked the commitment ring off my finger, ran outside and threw it into the lake. My relationship with Brad was over! Devastated, I walked through the next few days unable to feel anything but rage.

One day shortly afterward, I wandered into a bookstore. When I turned to leave, I accidently brushed against a book and knocked it on the floor. Picking it up, I noticed the title: *Women Who Love Too Much*, by Robin Norwood. Curious, I bought it, went home, and scoured the pages for answers to why I always picked drunken losers and ended up being the bigger loser.

Ms. Norwood explained how women from alcoholic homes choose men like their fathers and keep creating and reliving the same pain over and over. That was me! This pattern was ruining my life. I needed help.

The next morning I dragged myself out of bed. Without makeup, my eyes puffy and red, I slipped out of the house and drove to a nearby church where someone had told me they had one of those twelve-step meetings. As bad as I looked, a kind, smartly dressed woman met me at the door, smiled, and said, "Honey, things will get better." I grabbed onto those words like a drowning person about to go down for the last time grabs onto a life preserver.

8

Recovery

I began attending twelve-step recovery meetings to help me understand why I kept choosing alcoholic relationships. The early meetings were like Chinese stir-fry dishes: so much in them and all mixed up. I would leave the meetings confused, shaking my head. What did they mean when they said we should quit trying to control the drinking and stay out of the alcoholic's business? Were these people from outer space? If they had any idea of the hell I'd been through they might understand why I *had* to stop the drinking. In my mind, the drinking *was* the problem, and the only way I could be happy was to control it.

Over time, I'd find out why they were suggesting a 'hands off' policy, but at the beginning my nerves were shot, I barely focused on what was being said, and I couldn't make much sense out of any of it. My body showed up but my mind hung out in the past, obsessing over my failed relationships.

At first I said very little, but after a few months, when I felt more comfortable, I became a motormouth. I talked and talked and talked, unable to shut up. Years of frustration and pain over my father's drinking and my failed alcoholic relationships gushed out of me like water bursting through an old dam. I needed someone to understand and hear what I'd been through, and I found those listening ears at the recovery meetings. People nodded and understood because they'd had the same experiences. How comforting it was to find emotionally supportive people who truly grasped my suffering.

As I attended more meetings and shook the cobwebs out of my cluttered mind, I began to gain more insight into how my father's drinking and sexual abuse had negatively impacted my life. I could see how I kept going after one alcoholic man after another in a futile attempt to get the love I never received from my father. In recovery, they refer to this as going to an empty well for water, or going to a hardware store for a loaf of bread. I certainly had been doing that, and it had gotten me nowhere.

I could also see how my sexual abuse set me up for additional problems. From an early age, the rights to my body had been stolen by men. My body no longer belonged to me, and as a result, whoever wanted it could have it. This is what childhood sexual abuse creates: an inability to set healthy adult sexual boundaries. As a child, I blamed myself for the abuse, as most victims do, and developed low self-esteem, which further contributed to my putting up with unacceptable behavior. Not liking myself, I was desperate to get love and approval from someone else to prove that I was okay – lovable.

Before recovery, I secretly thought something was wrong with me. The choices I made, the feelings I had, and my actions were not those of a sane individual. None of my relationships worked out, and I drowned in a sea of self-pity and bitterness. What a relief to find out I wasn't crazy and didn't need to be shipped to the loony farm – that my actions merely reflected an alcoholic, abusive upbringing.

This new awareness opened a floodgate of pent-up emotions. One minute I raged, furious at my father, and the next moment I was in tears, feeling utterly depressed. I felt I had been doomed to a lonely life, devoid of a healthy relationship. During these difficult emotional ping-pong swings, I clung to the program slogan 'This too shall pass'. I identified easily with newcomers to the meeting who sat in the corner, trying to be invisible, while tears streamed down their cheeks.

The experienced women at the meeting encouraged me to get a sponsor, a woman who could teach me the principles and steps of recovery. I chose the first lady who smiled at me and said hello. Her name was Denise, and she had been in recovery for five years. Denise agreed to be my sponsor, but when we met she spent all our time talking about her problems, going on and on, and I didn't hear any solutions, just problems. That was all right with me because I wasn't too serious about this sponsor stuff and had only gotten one because I was supposed to.

After a year of not making much progress and feeling stuck in my pain, I knew I needed to work the steps of recovery. Denise was not taking me through the steps, so I fired her and hired a new sponsor named Mary. She was an old-timer, a no-nonsense woman who had been in recovery for many years. I heard around the tables to 'pick a winner', which meant finding a sponsor who had what I wanted. Mary seemed to fit the bill, as she had a strong grasp of the principles of recovery and exuded a serenity that I was lacking.

Mary and I met on a weekly basis to talk about recovery. She began with Step 1: 'We admitted we were powerless over alcohol, that our lives had become unmanageable' (adapted from *Alcoholics Anonymous*). She asked me, "In what way has your life been unmanageable?" I bristled at her question, feeling insulted, and curtly replied, "I don't know." Although I had experienced a series of disastrous relationships, my life was definitely not *unmanageable*. I saw myself as superwoman, a capable and strong individual, able to accomplish anything. My fragile ego kept me from admitting that I was incapable of managing my own life or anyone else's.

I'm sure this was not the first time Mary had run into resistance from a sponsee, but she remained patient and addressed the first part of Step 1: powerlessness. Mary stressed the importance of realizing that we cannot control the alcoholic, that we are powerless over his or her drinking. Being very stubborn, I rejected this idea also. After all, I had controlled the drinking of a couple of my alcoholics: I got Leo to stop drinking for five days when we took a camping trip around Lake Superior, and I talked Bob, a professor I briefly dated, into cutting back on his drinking when we were out with others. As soon as we arrived home, however, Bob guzzled down the booze, but at least he didn't do it in public. My denial was strong and, like an old comfortable coat, I was unwilling to discard it.

I thought the problem had been with the alcoholics in my life. *I* was fine. If the alcoholics had just listened to what I said and quit drinking, everything would have been great. And how could I be powerless over other people when, as a psychologist, clients came to me every day seeking answers to their problems. I felt powerful, almost God-like, in my ability to change others' lives.

Mary began chipping away at my denial like a woodworker carefully carving a statue. She explained how my unmanageability was reflected in my continual choice of alcoholic partners. She asked me how I was going to be happy if I kept choosing addicted men.

Mary also pointed out that my deep love for Leo was not enough to keep him from going to the bar rather than visiting me in the hospital. And even though I tried for years to persuade my father to quit drinking by pleading, loving, and scolding him, it didn't do any good. Mary asked, "How many alcoholics have you been able to get to stop drinking?" I had to be honest. "None." My wall of denial was beginning to crumble, but I was obstinate and it took many more years before I *truly* admitted I was powerless over alcoholics.

9

Therapy

Several years ago I attended a Lifespan Integration Workshop in Oakland, California, for continuing education. Lifespan Integration is a therapy technique that is used for healing past traumas. At the workshop, the presenter, Peggy Pace, asked for a volunteer to demonstrate the technique. Excited about the prospect of receiving free therapy, I quickly raised my hand. Peggy called me to the front of the room and asked me to recall a trauma from my childhood. A queasy feeling in my stomach instantly arose. I told Peggy I wanted to work on the sexual abuse by my father.

She guided me back to the time of the abuse and told me to bring into the scene someone who could help resolve the problem. Peggy suggested I might bring in a child protection worker, a policeman, my mother, or my adult self. I chose to bring my adult self into the setting with my little girl. She asked if that adult had anything to say to her father. My chest tightened as rage built up inside me like a volcano rumbling under pressure. I began to tremble and "If you ever touch her again, I'll kill you" erupted like hot lava from my mouth, shocking even me. I had no idea I was carrying that much hatred and anger toward my father.

After the workshop, I made a commitment to go to therapy and deal with my sexual abuse. I had unfinished business to take care of. The rage toward my father and other sexual abusers had been buried deep inside, and I was like a ticking time bomb ready to explode, just like I did at the workshop. I wanted to get in touch with my anger, release it, and heal.

I chose a female therapist named Lynn, whom I knew from our local psychological association meetings. Like me, Lynn was trained in Eye Movement Desensitization Reprocessing (EDMR), a form of psychotherapy developed by Dr. Francine Shapiro to resolve trauma-related disorders with the use of bilateral brain stimulation through eye movements, tones, or tapping.

The therapy work was not easy. It was emotionally draining to relive the past. But Lynn was supportive and gently led me through repeated EMDR sessions to resolve my pain and anger. I cried, raged, shook, rocked in my chair, and felt sick to my stomach as I emotionally purged, vomiting up all the past pain. My body developed mysterious aches and pains in my neck and back, and I contracted pneumonia for the first time in my life. Supposedly, the lungs are connected to grief, and surely I was grieving the loss of my little girl's innocence. At times I felt like I wouldn't get through the therapy, but I did.

I recall early on in therapy, during one of the sessions on my father, how I sobbed and cried out from the depths of my soul, "I just want him to love me!" That little girl was in so much pain. After about a year in therapy, the feelings began to lessen. I could talk about the abuse without feeling the heart-stabbing pain that had accompanied it in the past. I accepted that my abusers did the best they could under the circumstances. My negative attitude toward men was diminishing as my heart began to thaw. The abuse was in the past. It was over – and I was okay.

As a therapist and survivor of childhood sexual abuse, I believe therapy is important in healing the trauma. The consequences of childhood sexual abuse can be long lasting and disruptive to healthy adult functioning. Some advise 'Just move on. Forget about it', but it's my experience that before we can move on we need to deal with unresolved emotions, post-traumatic stress, addictions, and dissociative tendencies. Relationship difficulties, sexual problems, depression, and anxiety all need to be addressed. Survivors can use help in uncovering, expressing, and processing their anger in order to move toward personal empowerment. Help is also needed in developing skills for finding and maintaining healthy, supportive relationships.

10

Betrayal

As a consequence of my twelve-step program and therapy, my life became more peaceful, but I missed the rush of adrenaline that comes from all the ups and downs of relating to an alcoholic. Being surrounded by alcoholics my entire life, I had grown accustomed to the disturbing yet familiar chaos that accompanies addiction. I didn't feel alive unless I was bouncing up and down on an emotional roller coaster. I missed the drama and, like a dog returning to its vomit, I started another alcoholic relationship.

One night when I was sitting in the Diamond Bar, two men entered and took a seat at the bar directly opposite me. One was about five foot eight, slim, and wearing a blue jogging suit. On his head was a white yacht cap with a little visor and black anchor emblem on the front. He drew my attention; he didn't look like a local guy. I watched as a couple of men approached him at the bar to say hello. He became animated as he chatted with the two men, laughing and joking. There was a certain charisma about this man, and I wanted to meet him. I felt a magnetic draw to him, like that 'some enchanted evening, you will see a stranger across a crowded room' feeling.

I asked the bartender who he was and he said, "Oh, that's Rocky and his business partner, Tom. He just flew into town on his private plane from downstate. He's a realtor and land developer and owns a great deal of wilderness property in the UP." He sounded like an interesting man, and I really wanted to meet him, but it was late and I was tired, so I left the bar and headed home.

A week later I was at the university gym working out. As I exited the women's locker room, fresh from my shower, there stood Rocky outside the door. I was stunned.

"Excuse me," he said. "Did you see a little dark-haired twelve-year-old girl in there?"

"Yes," I replied, gulping back my surprise.

"Well, that's my daughter, Jamie. Could you please go back in and tell her to hurry up because her daddy's waiting for her?" I said okay and headed back in.

When I came out, he asked, "Do you work at the University?"

"Yes," I said. "I'm a psychologist in the counseling center."

"Oh," Rocky replied. "I'm a single dad who likes to stay active. Would you be interested in going hiking sometime so I can show you some beautiful waterfalls in the area?"

I couldn't believe he was asking me to do something. Trying not to act surprised, I coolly replied, "Sure, that sounds like fun."

"Can you give me your phone number so I can call you?"

I gave him my number and then his daughter came out. He said goodbye and they left. My heart was in overdrive. Not only did I meet Rocky, but he had asked me out.

A couple of days later, Rocky called and we went hiking together that weekend. He was like Davy Crockett in his knowledge of the woods. Skillfully, he led me along woodland paths to babbling brooks and gorgeous waterfalls. I fell in love with the beauty of the UP and liked the man who was showing it to me. Rocky was intelligent, charming, self-confident, funny and friendly – the complete package. Although he was eighteen years older than I was, the age difference didn't bother me because he was fit and active, and I gravitated toward older men and father figures anyway. Rocky and I hiked, cross-country skied, dined out, made love, and flew around Michigan in his private plane. His exciting world became my world, and I was not alone anymore.

Rocky had to travel downstate frequently to attend to business in his main office. If I was free, I'd go with him. More often than not, however, I had to work, so we were separated a lot. When he visited Marquette, he liked to be carefree and to party. He had to have his beer in the evenings, but that didn't disturb me because he was funny when he drank. At the time, I didn't think he had a drinking problem, but in retrospect I see how I was in denial and turned a blind eye to his excessive boozing.

One night he banged on my front door flat-out drunk. I was flattered that when he needed someone, he came to *me*. I helped him out of his clothes, put him to bed, and nursed him through his morning hangover. I still didn't think he had a drinking problem, for he was too successful. He flew a plane and ran a multimillion-dollar business. He wasn't like my dad, who passed out every night in his chair, or the bum lying on a park bench with an empty whiskey bottle next to him.

While I loved Rocky and enjoyed his company, I was frustrated with our one-sided love life. He initiated the sex, and it was over quickly – a 'wham, bam, thank you, ma'am' experience. He didn't bother to pleasure me or be concerned about my satisfaction. Consequently, I never got enough sex because I was not physically fulfilled. One night, when I was feeling horny, I put my arms around him in bed and said, "Do you want to be close tonight?" He pushed me away abruptly and said, "What's wrong with you? Are you a nymphomaniac? We just had sex two nights ago." His words tore through my fragile heart. I was too shocked and hurt to respond. He uttered a low grunt, turned over, and fell asleep, while I lay there wide awake and confused. *Is something wrong with me? Am I oversexed?*

In reality, I was simply sexually frustrated. I was not orgasmic, and my body craved to be touched, fondled, and stimulated and not just be used as a sperm depository. His accusation that I was a nymphomaniac shamed me into silence. I certainly wasn't going to bring up the topic again and be humiliated. I loved Rocky and was eager to please him. If that meant going along with how and when he wanted to have sex, so be it. Just having our bodies intertwined felt comforting to me. I wanted more, but settled for less, ignoring my needs.

I was thirty-five years old and had been dating Rocky for well over a year when my younger sister, Peg, called. She was married and living in Philadelphia. "We're having some marital problems," Peg told me. "I need to get away for a couple of days." I replied, "Well, Easter is next Sunday. Why don't you come for the weekend?" She was thrilled and said she'd be there. I felt close to Peg and looked forward to seeing her. Family was important to me!

Peg arrived on Good Friday and I took her to dinner at the Crow's Nest, a restaurant on the top floor of a downtown hotel overlooking Lake Superior. Unbeknownst to me, Rocky had just flown in from downstate and was having dinner there with his business partner. He came over to say hello and I introduced him to my sister. Rocky invited us to spend the weekend at his place. I asked Peggy if that would be all right with her and she said it would. So we all headed out to his house in the woods. We did some hiking, cooked nice meals, and relaxed. Sunday night Rocky and I had sex, which capped off a perfect weekend.

On Monday morning I had to return to work. Peg wanted to hang around for another day, so Rocky kindly offered to show her around the area. After work, I called Peg and she told me, "We had a great time, and I'm going to stay over one more night." I suggested she have Rocky drive her into town so the two of us might visit. Rocky lived far out in the woods, so I stayed in town during the work-week. She replied, "No, I'm going to bed early. Rocky has already made plans to show me some sights early in the morning." I told her goodnight and said I'd call her on Tuesday, grateful that Rocky was taking such good care of her.

On Tuesday, I called Peg and she said she planned on staying over one more night. My antenna went up and an uneasy, unsettled feeling came over me. I confronted my sister.

"Peggy, what's going on with you and Rocky?"

"Nothing," she replied.

"Well, you came to visit *me* and you're spending all your time with Rocky."

"He's just being nice and showing me the sights while you work," Peggy answered.

I asked to talk to Rocky but she said he was outside chopping wood.

The next day Peg called and said, "Rocky is driving me to the airport. I'm heading home." Feeling quite relieved, I told her goodbye and wished her a safe trip.

I tried unsuccessfully to reach Rocky by phone on Wednesday and Thursday. The weekend was coming up, and we usually spent it together. *Something is wrong! He hasn't called since I kissed him goodbye on Monday.* In desperation, I drove out to his place in the woods, but he wasn't home. I left a note asking him to call me.

I phoned again early the next morning, and Jamie, Rocky's daughter, answered. Jamie had been staying at a friend's house for the past few days and had just returned home. Her first words to me were, "Who is Peg?"

"Why are you asking?" I said.

"Oh, Daddy just said he was heading into town to meet a woman named Peg at the Ramada Inn," was Jamie's response. My heart dropped into my toes. Jamie had inadvertently let the cat out of the bag.

I was devastated. Peg had lied! She was sneaking around behind my back with Rocky. *How could she do this to me? She's my sister! How could they both betray me this way?* I felt like someone had kicked me in the stomach and left me dead on the street. My chest tightened up as the tears began to flow. My heart was once again shredded.

Over the next several weeks, Peg made no effort to call. She was, quite naturally, avoiding me. I heard that she had left her husband and moved in with Rocky. He was her ticket out of an unhappy marriage. They started appearing together all over town, and I began hiding out. I was embarrassed and heart-broken that my younger sister had betrayed me and stolen my boyfriend. Although I was mad at both of them, I was more upset with Peg, because she was family. In retrospect, I realize I had chosen one more alcoholic that couldn't be trusted.

After Peggy and Rocky's betrayal, I found it difficult to go on with my life, acting as if everything was all right. My world had collapsed. Sadness enveloped me like a dense, heavy fog. Having lost the one person I truly loved, I felt empty and alone. Walking through my days in a haze, I obsessed over the two of them being together. Nothing felt real, my heart ached so badly. One of my friends offered me some marijuana, and I smoked it to try to block out the pain. On the evenings and weekends all I did was cry and get high. I was a mess and needed help.

Part III

Moving On

The important thing is that men should have a purpose in life.
It should be something useful, something good.
The Dalai Lama

The Convent

After we've dealt with the effects of childhood abuse by breaking the secret and uncovering the shame, we then have the task of moving on. Recovery is not only about resolving the psychological issues posed by addictions, low self-esteem, and depression, but going on to live creative, productive, deeply satisfying lives. We are meant to be happy.

There is a story about a father who gave his young son a big pile of manure for Christmas. Immediately, the boy started digging through the pile, flinging manure here and there. His father stopped him and asked, "What are you doing?" The boy replied, "With such a big pile of manure, there must be a pony in here somewhere." Just like the little boy, after we plow through the shit of abuse and recover from its consequences, we need to find the pony or gift within. What doesn't kill us (physically, emotionally, or spiritually) makes us stronger. The human spirit is resilient and *can* find a gift within any of life's disturbing events. Often a sense of purpose or a call to give to others is evoked through an experience of the 'dark night of the soul'.

Look at Oprah Winfrey, a woman raised in poverty in rural Mississippi to a teenage single mother. At the age of nine she was raped, and at fourteen she became pregnant, only to have her son die in infancy. She was not beaten down by these early experiences but went on to become a billionaire and a wildly successful talk show host, producer, and philanthropist. Her *Oprah Winfrey Show* has positively affected the lives of so many people she is considered one of the most influential women of our times.

Then there is Nelson Mandela, South Africa's first black president. After leading a long campaign against the apartheid government of South Africa, he was arrested and spent twenty-seven years in an isolated prison cell. Oprah and Nelson found their gifts after extreme hardship, and shared them with others. Of course, we are not all called to such greatness as Oprah Winfrey or Nelson Mandela, but we do have our own unique gift to give to the world. The modern artist Pablo Picasso said, "The meaning of life is to find your gift. The purpose of life is to give it away."

Our gift can take many forms. For some, it's living a life of artistic expression through music, art, dance, or writing. Others find fulfillment in building a healthy relationship or being a devoted parent. Some women pour themselves into productive and fulfilling careers, while others find their own unique ways to serve. Being of service and loving God was my calling, and I knew this from an early age. That's why I entered the convent.

As a young Catholic child, I read all the books I could find on the lives of the saints, and I wanted to emulate their lives. As a teenager, I wanted to enter the convent but didn't get accepted. Then, in my early twenties, I began working on my master's degree at a Catholic university. My philosophy professor was a Polish Jesuit priest in his late fifties who was short in stature, wore glasses, and had balding gray hair. Father was an entertaining, animated, and engaging lecturer who, with his gestures and Polish accent, made Plato and Aristotle come to life. I admired him. He was such a good teacher: knowledgeable, friendly, and willing to help his students.

One day after class I approached Father to ask about a test question. He explained the question and then directed the conversation to a personal note. "What are you doing with your life?" he asked. I told him I had been working in the inner city of Cleveland and now wanted to get my master's degree in counseling so I could help others. He said, "I want to start a secular institute in Cincinnati and I'm looking for someone like you to help me get it going." I was flattered. He must have seen something in me that led him to invite me to join in such an important endeavor. He continued, "I've already founded secular institutes in Poland and Canada, and now I want to establish one in this city. Would you be interested in helping me?"

A secular institute is a modern religious order in which women take the traditional vows of poverty, chastity, and obedience, live among the people, and serve, but do not wear nuns' clothing. The concept was appealing to me, for I had no interest at this point in my life of living in an isolated, stuffy, cloistered convent away from the world. I had no idea why Father had singled me out from the other female students, but I did see how my life had come full circle. I wanted to be a nun, and a modern order would suit me. I said yes. A door had opened, and I stepped through.

I recruited other young women to join us, and some of us lived together in a community house. I was the female director of the Institute, while Father was the overall head. On Christmas Eve, in a solemn ceremony in the rectory chapel, I made my permanent vows of poverty, chastity, and obedience. For seven years I dedicated myself to serving God through the Secular Institute, doing social work in the inner city and helping priests in local Catholic parishes. These were some of the happiest days of my life, and I committed to serving God as a nun until the day I died.

One morning, however, everything suddenly changed. The women in the Institute had been complaining about Father's controlling behavior, authoritarian style, and overbearing mannerisms. One said she hated his practice of snapping his fingers at us like we were dogs when he wanted our attention. I had to acknowledge that was something he did, but it never really fazed me, for I remained the obedient, loyal nun. I suggested to the women that they take the higher road and not talk about Father but rather pray for him.

This worked for a while until they once again became

frustrated and started griping. We were living in the early seventies, when the women's lib movement was in full swing with cries for liberation and equality, so I could understand where these women were coming from. They were not used to cowering before a male authority figure and did not embrace the vow of obedience like I did.

After months of listening to the women's endless bellyaching, I decided to talk to Father about it at our morning meeting. I had avoided doing this because I didn't want the women's criticism to upset him, but he had advised me to bring any problems in the community to him. He was in charge and he needed to know.

The next morning at our meeting I said, "Father, I want to tell you that some of the women have been coming to me complaining about the amount of control you have over us." His face turned scarlet and he instantly went into attack mode, like a cornered wild tiger.

"*You* are going to ruin the Institute," he yelled.

What's he talking about? I'm not the one complaining.

"You are from the devil. Get out of here! I never want to work with you again," he screamed.

Stunned, I tried to defend myself and stammered, "Fa-Father, I didn't say this, and I'm not the one complaining."

"Get out," he shrieked. "You have turned against me and ruined everything."

My heart sank! Somehow I had become the enemy, and he wanted nothing to do with me. I sat paralyzed, unable to move or say a word. Suddenly, he rose from his chair, pointed to the door, and commanded, "GET OUT!" I got up, hung my head, and exited, feeling like Judas. I had betrayed my master.

I staggered out of the building, blindsided by his painful rejection and unable to make sense of it. *What just happened? How could I work with Father every day for seven years and then be cruelly cast aside as if I were an evil person?* For so many years he had fulfilled the role of a good father, providing me with the safe environment that I never had growing up. Now he was casting me aside with complete disregard. I sat in my car sobbing uncontrollably, tears dripping onto my white, now wet, blouse. My life had come to an end! When the tears finally subsided, I wiped my red, swollen eyes and drove home.

From the appearance of my face, the women knew something drastic had happened. Painfully, I recounted the disturbing details of my conversation with Father and the fact that he had disowned me. The women were happy and rejoiced in finally being free from Father's iron grip. As they reveled in their newfound freedom, I sank into a deep depression.

Attending church that year on Christmas Eve, the anniversary of the day I had made my vows, I wept through the service, lost in my aloneness. Nothing made sense. Father had run the Institute; it was his dream, and now, like a boat without a rudder, our community drifted aimlessly at sea. Did I want to keep the community afloat? I felt I had to because I had recruited the women, lived with some of them, and formed a close bond. I couldn't just abandon them.

I stayed and worked with the women for another year, even though my heart had departed. I trudged through my days like a mindless robot, repetitively putting one foot in front of the other, while my gut roiled with disillusionment and bitterness. All my past trust issues with men bubbled to the surface. How could I trust anyone again when my confidant – a priest, a man of God – had unfairly turned on me, betraying me in an instant?

At the time, the ordeal seemed like a terrible tragedy. But now, many years later, I see how it marked the beginning – although a shaky, tentative beginning – of breaking free from the chains that had bound me and reclaiming my own life and spirituality. I had been born into Catholicism, attended eighteen years of private Catholic schools, and spent seven years in the convent without ever questioning my beliefs. I was a faithful lamb that followed the shepherd. But now my inherited belief system and its representatives were failing me, and I had to look elsewhere for my answers: to discover my own truths and spiritual way.

12

Alice

Alice entered my life a few years after I left the convent and began dating one alcoholic after another. I first met her at a friend's birthday party. She was an unassuming, simple-looking woman in plain dress, with pure white hair pulled back in a little bun from her tanned and chiseled face – someone you'd hardly notice in a crowd. People, however, flocked around her at the party, as she drew everyone's attention. *What do they find interesting about this woman?* I wondered. I kept my distance, while continuing to observe her from afar. My friend Melanie told me she did some kind of spiritual work, and while I was curious, I had had enough religion, churches, and priests to last a lifetime. I avoided her at the party until the very end, when I merely said, "Hello."

After my sister and Rocky's betrayal, I was devastated and in severe emotional pain. I didn't know what to do but I knew I needed help. Then I remembered meeting Alice. I decided to phone her.

"Can you come for six days?" she asked. I was shocked. Six days. I didn't know if I had the energy to last even one day.

"I need that time to really help people," Alice said.

A red flag went up in my mind. "You're not going to lay some religious trip on me, are you?" I shot back.

"No, I'll help you find yourself," she calmly replied. That satisfied me and I told her I'd be there the next day. I had no idea what she did or how she was going to help me, but I was desperate and needed to be out of my pain.

Early the next morning, I drove fifty miles to the sleepy little town of Munising, nestled between the hills and shore of Lake Superior. Alice met me at the door of her charming two-story home. Polished dark hardwood framed the doorways and windows, and the staircase was fashioned from the same wood. I noticed there was no television or radio, just a piano sitting in a corner of the living room. A small fire burned in the fireplace, giving the room a cozy feeling. A quiet, peaceful energy permeated the house, and I instantly felt comfortable and at home.

Since Alice didn't charge for her work, I had brought nuts, fruit, cheese, and bread for our meals. She put the food away and we settled in the living room – I on the couch and Alice in a well-worn, comfortable-looking upholstered chair.

She began to speak. "I depend completely on my *team* to guide me." Her team consisted of holy ones from various religions: Jesus, Mary, Krishna, Lao-tse, the Holy Ghost, and St. Peter, to name a few. She closed her eyes, asked for help from her team, and came up with an outline for the six days. It involved looking at my relationship with self and others, rebirthing, past lives and life reading. I didn't believe in reincarnation and the rest was Greek, but I decided to suspend judgment and see what happened.

Alice started with a rebirthing session, which involves taking a person back through the birth to release any trauma related to it. She had me lie on a blue blanket in a fetal position on the floor in front of the fireplace. She then directed me to go to the time right before my physical birth as she counted from one to one hundred. My first awareness was of Mom and Dad being at a New Year's Eve party. Mom's water broke. Dad was too drunk to take her to the hospital so a woman friend drove her. The doctor, who had been called in from another party, examined Mother and said, "You'll be ready to deliver in a couple of hours." He then left to take a nap in the doctors' room to sleep off his drinking.

Several hours later he returned, examined Mom again, and said, "You're still not ready." Mom, alone and in hard labor, lost what little composure she had left and screamed, "You said I'd be ready in a couple of hours!" The doctor lost his temper and responded, "Okay, if that's the way you want it, we'll wheel you in and *take* the baby."

Mom felt guilty, because she knew she wasn't ready to deliver. So when the anesthesiologist administered the ether, she tried not to breathe too deeply. Finally, she took a deep breath and lost consciousness. Now she was unable to help with the birthing process and the doctor had to use forceps. He had trouble. My head crowned, but my shoulders were broad, making the birthing difficult. The doctor cursed and, thinking I was a boy, said, "Jesus Christ, he's stuck." Eventually, he managed to maneuver me out of the birth canal, injuring my shoulders in the process. I cringed as I thought about this doctor angrily ripping me from my mother's womb. Painfully, I entered the world on New Year's Day through the hands of an irritable doctor with alcohol on his breath.

I was astounded by all this information, not knowing whether it was true or if I had made it up. I've been told I have a rich imagination, so maybe I'd created the whole birth scenario. Nevertheless, my birthing 'story' fit well with my life experiences. The pieces of the puzzle were coming together. During my life, both of my shoulders have dislocated through sports at least fifty times. Were they weakened through the birthing process? And what about the doctor who had been drinking and forced my delivery? He was in a position of power and misused that power. So did my father, Ronnie, and my two bosses who sexually abused me. My early life was replete with men taking charge and victimizing me. My birth dynamics had been replaying over and over in my life.

On a spiritual level, I wondered if my relationship with Jesus was affected by the doctor using His name in vain during my birth. Alice told me that Jesus was my main guide, but throughout my life I had wrestled with an on-and-off relationship with Him. At times, I'd feel extremely close to Jesus, and other times I'd distance myself. *Did the doctor's cursing confuse my soul and contribute to my ever-changing relationship with Jesus?*

I found it all very interesting at the time, and was even more intrigued when, years later, my sister, who is a nurse, told me it was true. She said, "Mom didn't tell you the details of your birth because she didn't want to upset you, but what you remembered actually happened." I was astonished by my sister's confirmation. How could I have known all those specifics of my birth? Could there be a consciousness within us that is aware of being in the womb and experiencing birth? I think there is.

Three days into my work with Alice my paternal grandmother died. I left Alice's house and flew home for the funeral. Everyone loved Grandma and many were crying at her viewing. As I approached the casket, holding my mother's arm, I sensed Grandma's presence floating above the coffin. Then I clearly heard these words: "Tell them not to cry or be sad. I am free from pain and happy." Excitedly, I told those around me what I just heard, and Mom told me to be quiet, I was embarrassing her. I was so wide open from Alice's work that I was able to communicate with my Grandma's spirit. No matter what Mom said, I knew Grandma was there and she talked to me.

After the funeral I returned to Alice's house and we started doing some past life regressions. The process involves taking a person back to a prior life through hypnosis, deep relaxation or, in Alice's case, a symbol session. With symbols, a person relaxes and then says whatever comes to mind: a thought, a feeling, a mental picture. Alice and I exchanged symbols, back and forth, for about twenty minutes as I became very relaxed.

Alice explained before we started that the purpose of a regression is to see what we experienced in a prior life and find out how that life is affecting our current life. Often the people we know in our present life we have known in a past life, and the problems we have today are connected to unresolved issues from that former life.

That certainly was the case with my sister Peggy. One of my symbols took me to a life as a young woman in England where Peg and I were together as we are in this incarnation. She was my sister and I betrayed *her* by sleeping with her husband. After the regression, Alice said, "Your current experience is merely karmic payback for this past life." I wasn't sure I believed in karma or past lives, but the regression enabled me to get a different perspective on the betrayal. Maybe this *was* payback! Alice said, "We have been on both sides of an issue in our former lives: the betrayer and the one betrayed, the abuser and the one abused. We experience different life situations for the soul's learning, and we encounter one another in this life for soul development. There is no need to judge anyone." This perspective helped me release some of my resentment toward Peg and Rocky.

In another past life I was a woeful orphan boy living on the street. The abbot of a local monastery picked me off the street, fed, clothed, and sheltered me. He gave me the necessities of life but was unable to give me love. I met that abbot again. He was my father in this present life, but he still withheld his love. He had a chance to resolve his karma with me, but his addiction left him incapable of doing so.

Alice took me through a life as a Spanish priest who went to minister to and Christianize the American Indians. As I lived among the Indians, I was impressed with their community spirit and peaceful ways. These were wise people who honored the earth and each other. I wanted to learn more about their spiritual ways, so when they invited me to participate in one of their sacred peyote ceremonies, I accepted. After I ingested the peyote I saw a richly pulsating color spectrum. Beautiful colors! Then I had a transcendent experience of directly communicating with God and receiving deep insights into higher truths. After the ceremony, I believed that the sacred peyote was the key to the Indians' wisdom and serenity.

Alice told me, "In this life you have continued to search for ways to transcend ordinary consciousness, wanting to reenact your peyote experience with the Indians. That is why you were drawn to marijuana, thinking it would be a means to higher levels of consciousness." I thought about what weed did for me and realized it did not lead to a deeper spiritual experience. It helped me relax, let go of my worries, drop my inhibitions, enhance my enjoyment of music, increase my appetite, and sharpen my senses, but it did not lead to introspection and deeper spiritual insights. After I left Alice's house I never smoked marijuana again, for I knew it couldn't enhance my spiritual connection.

Alice received from her guides my life reading: an overview of the soul's evolution through time. I began as a bee, three million years ago. I evolved through the lower life forms to human life. My soul's basic 'definition', as Alice spoke of it, was to serve and be served. My choice in my present life was to flow with peace, love, and joy, and to resolve my karma.

Alice used the analogy of a ladder, which she called 'Jacob's Ladder', to indicate where we are on our spiritual journey. Each rung of the ladder represents a higher virtue: truth, unconditional love, service, creativity, humility, acceptance of life and death, sexuality and spirituality, honesty and nonjudgment. The goal is to work on each of these areas so that we become more virtuous, more God-like. Alice received a 'reading' from her team to see where I was with each of these attributes. She said, "You are not afraid to be honest with yourself and you are 91 percent honest with others. Your humility is at 80 percent, nonjudgment 50 percent, acceptance of life 100 percent, acceptance of death 75 percent, sexuality 60 percent, and creativity 90 percent."

The areas that needed to be worked on were judgment, sexuality, and acceptance of death. We started with judgment. I told Alice that judging others seemed to be inherent in the Hodge DNA. If we weren't criticizing outsiders, we were attacking each other. My alcoholic father was especially critical, pummeling us with his biting remarks. Cruel taunts and sarcasm pervaded our interactions.

Sarcasm comes from the Greek work *sarkasmos*, which means to tear flesh, and even though my family thought the bitter gibes were amusing, they often left gaping wounds. Not until I was grown and away from my family did I realize this was not the norm; other people didn't talk to one another this way. Today, I choose to be around people who are kind and gentle and refrain from derisive, cutting comments.

Along with the family dynamics, my religion also contributed to my judgmental behavior. The Catholic Church emphasized right and wrong, good and bad, the sinful. I was taught to examine my conscience each night and recall all the sins I had committed that day. Invariably, I'd fall short of the Church's expectations and beat myself up. I was a bad person. I lived in the dark, scary confessional box, beating my breast and repeatedly telling the priests the same sins. I judged myself harshly, which lowered my feelings of self-worth, and to compensate, I judged others unmercifully, trying to convince myself of my superiority.

Learning how to release judgment of self and others would be difficult, an uphill battle, because the tendency to judge was so deeply rooted in my character. Judgment often leads to resentments, and holding on to resentments is like drinking poison and waiting for the other person to die. It only hurts us! The poison was starting to taste too bitter in my mouth. I knew I was still carrying some resentment toward Peg and Rocky.

Alice emphasized that being on a spiritual path meant one had to forgive and release all judgment of others. She had me visualize through the eyes of God my sister Peg, Rocky, and others I felt had harmed me, which enabled my heart to soften and the process of forgiveness to begin. What a relief to get that resentment monkey off my back! I still grappled, however, with quieting those hidden, critical thoughts that sometimes held my mind captive – everyday experiences like someone cutting in front of me in line or driving too slowly or leaving the toilet seat up. I had a long way to go to sainthood.

It didn't surprise me that my sexuality needed to be worked on, as I was well aware that my past sexual abuse had created problems. In her reading, Alice described my sexuality as a decayed, rotting cat covered with layers of rocks, dirt, and ashes. The cat's jaw was dislocated and it had a broken front paw. I was appalled at Alice's graphic description, but she was right on. My sexual self had been broken and buried under layers of personal blame and shame from the abuse.

Not until I started writing this book and began therapy was I able to excavate those painful memories and realize the abuse was not my fault.

Alice stressed the need for each person to accept life and death completely – 100 percent. She said I had only accepted death 75 percent, so we needed to work on my complete acceptance. To do that, she took me to a past life as a Buddhist Tibetan monk living in a monastery in the Himalayan mountains. For the first fifty years of my life I studied and meditated. After that, a small group of younger monks was assigned to me for mentoring. We studied together, meditated, sang Tibetan mantras, chanted and played our musical instruments: cymbals, brass horns, and trumpets.

I mentored the young monks for many years, until I grew old and frail. As holy monks, we were able to will ourselves through our deaths; we were able to decide *when* we would pass over. My time had come to let go of my body. I walked up into the mountains to a small lean-to, sat down in the lotus position to meditate, and waited to be liberated from my body. Suddenly an image of the Buddha floated toward me with outstretched hands. When he got about six inches from my heart, my spirit floated out through the center of my chest, leaving me with an indescribable feeling of ecstasy. After this event, I no longer feared death, for I saw it merely as a transition to a state of pure joy and bliss.

A couple of years after this regression, a professor friend made a trip to Nepal. Upon his return, he gifted me with a traditional Tibetan belt that monks wore during ritual ceremonies. I asked, "What made you pick this out for me?" He replied, "Oh, I just thought you might like it." I asked him if he knew I had a past life as a Buddhist Tibetan monk. "No, that's quite amazing," he replied. "Yes, it is," I responded. "Thank you for such a significant gift. I will always treasure it."

When my six days with Alice had come to an end, I didn't want to leave. Her house had become a peaceful refuge from my troubled world. Alice was my lifeline. She plucked me out of the depths of despair and placed me on a path of healing. I went to her to get help with my feelings of loss and betrayal, and I received that help and so much more. Alice opened my eyes to an entirely different way of viewing life, introducing me to a whole new world of spiritual understanding. She shook up my way of seeing reality and I entered more fully into the mystery of life. I knew I'd be forever grateful for her help.

I continued to see Alice over the next seven years, and she became my spiritual teacher and dear friend. She was a very wise woman who was totally dedicated to helping others. It was so inspiring to see how fully she gave her life to God's work, and I wanted to do the same. I discovered a secret: find someone (or something) bigger than yourself and hook on to it. It will hoist you up. Hitch yourself to someone else's wagon and let them carry you along until you find your own wagon. Whatever you are – an aspiring actor, musician, artist, song writer, dancer – find winners in that area and learn from them.

I took clients and friends to see Alice so they could experience her work, and as I observed her working, I learned a great deal. I decided to open a holistic health center and address the body, mind, and spirit needs of my clients. Together with other practitioners – a nurse, a nutritionist, a massage therapist, and an energy worker – we formed a team to address the whole person.

I began integrating the spiritual work I had learned from Alice into my therapy sessions, including past life regression work.

I found that it didn't make any difference whether or not my clients believed in reincarnation or past lives, they could still benefit from a past life regression. When clients looked at their lives and issues from a distance through a past life, they were able to get a better perspective. It was amazing to see how the past life memories my clients came up with, whether real or imagined, were so instrumental in their healing process. I'm convinced that past life regression therapy is a powerful therapeutic tool.

My own spiritual journey and service to others became the focus of my life. Alice was a big part of my journey, but sadly she passed over seven years after I met her. I was devastated by her passing, however, shortly after she left, I was comforted by contact with her from the spirit world. I could hear her voice and guidance in my head, especially when I was doing spiritual work with my clients.

13

Snake Medicine

One day my girlfriend Sally mentioned she was planning to attend a Native American powwow in Rapid River, Michigan, and asked if I wanted to go. As a child, I was always fascinated by Indians. I liked Tonto better than the Lone Ranger, and when we played Cowboys and Indians, I wanted to be the Indian. As a Girl Scout I learned Indian dancing and heard about the Native American rain dance. I'd go outside and do my toe-heel dancing, gazing up at the sky, waiting for rain to fall.

When I was eighteen, my family and I took a trip to the Grand Canyon. Our tour guide was a teenage Hopi Indian with long, coal-black hair and handsome, chiseled facial features. I was mesmerized by his appearance as well as his love of nature and his quiet, peaceful demeanor. In typical teenage fashion, I fell instantly in love with him and fantasized about the two of us riding off together on a painted pony. Even at this young age I knew there was something special about Native Americans.

"Yes," I replied to Sally's invitation, "I'd love to go."

At the powwow, we listened to the drumming and singing and watched the Native dancers in their traditional regalia. Men wore beaded breastplate chokers with beautiful feathered bustles on their backs, colorful headdresses, leggings, and moccasins. Some of the women wore buckskin dresses with leggings and carried feathered ceremonial fans, while others were outfitted in colorful jingle dresses. I was delighted by the dancing and the drumming.

Since no drinking or drugs are permitted at powwows, the atmosphere was quite pleasant. There were a variety of booths set up for food and handmade Native items.

We feasted on greasy *fry bread* and perused the merchandise.

At one booth, the Native American vendor suggested we check out a much bigger powwow up north in Baraga later in the year. He told us, "They have a two-day spiritual gathering with elders who conduct talking circles and sweat lodges before the powwow begins."

Although I knew nothing about sweat lodges, as soon as he mentioned the words I felt a strong draw to participate in one. I made up my mind to attend the Baraga powwow.

Prior to the powwow, I'd had some unusual experiences with snakes. As a child, I loved to go to my grandparents' farm in the Kentucky hills and ride the horses, feed the animals, and play. I was relaxed at Grandma's and enjoyed a much welcomed respite from the turmoil at home. It was a place where my stomach wasn't always twisted in knots, waiting for the next crisis to occur.

I especially enjoyed being outdoors with the animals, but before I went out, Grandma always warned me to watch out for the snakes because some were poisonous. She repeated her warning so frequently that I developed a snake phobia and was terrified of seeing one. One day when I was nine, I was running barefoot through the field and looked down to see my foot about to land on a copperhead snake. I don't know how I did it or whether I had help from my guardian angel, but I jumped and stayed suspended in the air for about five feet until I landed beyond the snake.

My fear of snakes continued into my adult life and, like a bad nightmare, it wouldn't go away. It certainly didn't escape me that Freud, the father of psychoanalysis, saw the snake as a phallic symbol representing the penis and sexual drive. One Freudian interpretation of a snake is that it represents our relationship to sexuality and male figures. Given my sexual abuse by men, it surely made sense that I'd be afraid of them.

Whenever I saw a snake I'd panic, my heart beating wildly in my chest as I ran the other way. I couldn't relax when I was outdoors. I was always looking down, scanning left and right, fearful of seeing a snake. When I moved to the UP, I was elated to hear there were no poisonous snakes there. My mind reveled in thoughts of spending carefree time in the woods without fear. That joy was short-lived, however; when I spotted my first garter snake, I still felt petrified. Phobias are irrational – they don't make sense – and whether it was poisonous or not, to me it was still a dreaded *snake*.

One day some girlfriends invited me to go on a camping trip to the Porcupine Mountains in the western UP. Immediately, I thought about snakes. *I can't go. I might see a snake.* But my love of camping and desire to be with my friends overrode my anxiety, and I joined them. While hiking one day, I spotted a large pine snake slithering across the trail. I jumped and screamed. The other women asked what was wrong and I told them I had seen a big snake. They all shook their heads. None of them had seen it. I recalled Alice's words: "We bring into our lives that which we fear in order to release it." I wondered if that was what I was doing.

After I got home from camping, I felt I had to do something about my phobia. I was disgusted by my irrational fear and irritated by how it interfered with my enjoyment of nature. I wanted to get over it, to be rid of it, to no longer let it control my life, but I didn't know how to make that happen. Then I recalled reading about how Native Americans consider all creation sacred: the four legged, the tall standing ones, the winged, the waters, rocks, and creepy crawly ones, including snakes. *How could I be one with the Creator if I didn't accept all of His creatures?* I bowed my head and said a heartfelt prayer asking God to remove my phobia. Afterward, I went for a long walk in the woods with my dog Bryan.

When we returned, my body froze in terror at the sight of a five-foot long thick-bodied snake lying on my front porch blocking the entrance to my house. *Where did it come from? Why is it on my porch?* I had never seen a snake by my house or anywhere on my property in the seven years I had lived there. This was strange! I stood about twenty feet away watching the motionless snake basking in the warm August sun.

After a while I became impatient and wanted to get into the house, so I started throwing sticks up on the porch to get it to move. It crawled a few feet from the screen door and stopped. Gathering all the courage I could muster, I darted for the door and ran inside. Looking out, I saw the snake still lying in the same spot. I had to get it off my porch but I was sure it was going to turn and attack me. I later discovered that unless snakes are startled or cornered, they're as eager to get away from us as we are from them. But this snake wasn't going anywhere. It was just lying motionless on the porch, soaking up the heat of the sun.

I had to do something; I couldn't let it stay on my porch. I found a long-handled broom, reached out the door, and placed the straws behind the snake's tail until it slithered off the porch. It probably found refuge under my porch but at least I couldn't see it anymore. I took a deep breath, exhaled, and relaxed. It was over!

When I awoke the next morning and opened the front door, I was startled to see another snake, half the length of the first, lying on the porch. *What is going on?* I couldn't believe there was another snake on my porch. I stared at it through the front window of my cabin, forcing myself to look at it, to get comfortable with its presence. It had yellow and white longitudinal stripes against a brown background, with a slender body extending to a larger, oval-shaped head. The longer I gazed at it, the more relaxed I became. *This is a harmless creature. I don't need to be afraid of it.* Once again, I asked God to remove my fear, and as I did, the snake slowly crawled off the porch and disappeared in the grass.

Early the next morning I ran to the door to see if there were any more visitors. There weren't. The phone rang. It was my mother. As I talked to her on the remote phone, I wandered back to the door and saw another snake on the porch, a little smaller than the first two. It seemed like a whole family had nested near my house.

"Oh my God, Mom, there's a snake on my porch," I screamed into the phone.

"Well, go out and kill it," she said.

"I can't," I replied. "There's something going on with me and these snakes." My mom probably rolled her eyes and thought, "There goes my weird daughter."

After seeing three different snakes on the porch, I was petrified thinking about where the next one might appear. *Will it be in my house? Will it be in my bed?* The thoughts were horrifying.

The next morning, after thoroughly scanning the porch, I walked cautiously through the grass with my briefcase in my hand toward my truck, parked by the garden, about eighty yards from the house. It was locked and all the windows were rolled up tight. As I approached the truck and unlocked it, I looked down at my front left tire, which appeared low on air. My eyes were focused on the tire as I unlocked the door and slid into the bucket seat. Raising my head, I found myself staring straight into the eyes of the large snake, which was stretched across the dashboard, its head raised up above the steering wheel no more than a foot from my face. Hyperventilating, I leapt out of the truck in shock. *How did that snake get in my truck?* I stood by the truck trembling, realizing I had to get it out so I could go to work, and knowing I couldn't do it myself.

I called a neighbor who said she didn't like snakes but wasn't afraid of them and agreed to come and help. I handed her a broom and stood safely away, six feet up on a picnic table. She took several swipes at the snake and finally knocked it out the open truck door. The snake crawled back toward my porch. I thanked my neighbor and tore down the driveway, late for work. The rest of the day my mind was tormented with thoughts about the snakes. *What is going on? Why are they around me all of a sudden? Why won't they go away and leave me alone?*

The God of my childhood was a punishing, vindictive God, and I believed if bad things, like the snakes, were happening, I must have done something wrong. That evening, out of fear, I reviewed my life to see if something was amiss. The only thing I could think of was my relationship with Paul, a man I had recently been dating. Paul was extremely controlling and jealous, and the relationship was unhealthy. I needed to end it, but I hadn't because I didn't want to hurt him. Now it was time. I called him and told him it was over. After I hung up, I felt a sense of relief. With my distorted thinking, I believed I had appeased my avenging God and that would be the end of the snakes.

That weekend I packed my camping gear on my motorcycle and headed north into Canada for a much-needed break. I spent a renewing, peaceful weekend camping out in nature. All was right with the world, and my snake experiences were behind me. When I returned home, I drove to my girlfriend's house to pick up Bryan, my dog. Coming back, I made a large circle in the yard and parked the truck by the garden. As I walked through the grass to my cabin, I jumped back with a scream just before my foot landed on the big snake. My heart racing, I thought, *It's back!* Quickly I skirted around it and ran for the door while Bryan, oblivious to the drama, trotted after me.

Soon it began to drizzle, followed by a typical UP wind-driven downpour. I glanced out the front window and noticed that the snake had flipped over on its back, displaying its yellow belly. *How strange. Why is the snake lying like that in the hard rain? Why isn't it crawling to shelter?* I called a girlfriend who is psychic and asked if she knew why a snake would be lying on its back in the rain. She responded, "Elaine, I think the snake is dying, and you need to go out and help it pass over."

I was terrified by what she was asking me to do, but I believed her and knew I had to do it. I went outside, stood in the rain about ten feet from the snake, and peered at it. I didn't see any marks or injuries on it, but I asked God to help it pass over if it was dying. Before going to bed, I turned on the spotlight, looked outside, and saw the snake still lying there immobile. My inner voice told me it had died and I should bury it in the morning.

Upon awakening the next morning, I picked up the book I had been reading, *Medicine Woman,* by Lynn Andrews, opened it to my marker, and started reading the next chapter. Lynn was visiting a medicine woman in Canada to learn about the traditional ways. The elder woman told Lynn to go to a pond on her property and sit there until her spirit helper appeared. Lynn asked, "How will I know who my spirit helper is?" The woman replied, "You'll know."

Lynn sat patiently at the pond for hours with nothing happening. Then, sensing something, she turned to see that a rattlesnake had crawled up close to her. She froze like a statue, paralyzed, fearful that any movement might cause the snake to strike. Fighting to control her panic, she closed her eyes and asked God for help.

Upon opening her eyes, she watched as a butterfly touched down lightly on the snake's head and then flew over and tapped her on the forehead. With that, the snake turned and crawled away. Lynn knew that she had met her spirit helpers: the snake and the butterfly. She put some tobacco on the ground to give thanks and returned to the house.

I couldn't believe this was the next chapter in the book I was reading, for here I was dealing with my own snake experience. I shut the book, got dressed, and went outside to bury the snake. I gingerly touched it with the broom to be sure it was dead, and when I found it was I dug a hole about a foot deep, swept the snake onto a snow shovel, and put it in the hole. I filled the grave with dirt and placed a large piece of wood over it as a marker. Then I went into the woods, picked some wildflowers, and carefully arranged them around the grave. Finally, I took some tobacco and placed it on the ground, as Lynn had done.

As I stood reflecting over the grave, I heard a voice inside, which I believed was the spirit of the snake, say, "Our paths have crossed in order for me to help you. I gave up my life, allowing you to run over me with your truck, so that you may get over your fear." Upon hearing these words, I was shaken to my core. The snake had given up its life for me! A great feeling of love welled up in my heart and tears began streaming down my face as I sensed a deep healing within. The snake and I had become one. The snake was *my* spirit helper!

14

Sweat Lodge

My mind-boggling snake experiences fueled my desire to learn more about traditional Native spirituality. I also wanted to experience a sweat lodge, so I decided to go to the Baraga powwow. Arriving in my truck packed full with camping gear, I found a secluded spot and set up camp. Then I wandered around the grounds and happened upon some women sitting in a circle. They motioned for me to join them. An elder woman passed around an eagle feather, and as each woman received the feather, she spoke from her heart. Some deep words of wisdom were spoken which touched me profoundly. What a blessing!

After the women's talking circle, I strolled around the area trying to get more information about a sweat lodge. I soon found out that Indian ways are very informal. Information is exchanged through word of mouth – no billboards or loud-speaker announcements. I had no idea how I was going to find out about a sweat lodge. Then I fortuitously overheard two young Native women talking about heading over to the sweat lodge.

I followed them at a respectful distance into the woods. We came upon a small group of women who were busy building the lodge. It was a four-foot-high dome-shaped structure supported by willow branches and covered with tarps and blankets. A flap was left open on the east side to enter the lodge and, inside, cedar boughs had been placed on the ground. In the center was a two-foot deep circular hole that would hold the grandfather and grandmother hot stones. I approached a woman named Cathy who was directing the activities and asked, "Can I take part in the ceremony?" She replied, "Yes, of course, come back this evening."

At dusk I returned to the woods and found a few women

gathered around the lodge. Two were white women who had never been in a lodge, and the rest were Native Americans. Cathy was there, and she explained that the purpose of the lodge was to cleanse and purify ourselves both physically and spiritually. She then proceeded with some teachings about the four sacred Indian medicines – tobacco, cedar, sage, and sweet grass – and talked about how they are used for prayer, cleansing, and ceremonies.

Cedar is placed on the ground inside the sweat lodge, and when a person is outdoors fasting, cedar is placed in a protective circle around the individual.

Sage is used to remove negative energies and to cleanse sacred items. After an argument, or when moving into a new home, sage can purify the surroundings and clear out negativity. Both sage and sweet grass can be used in smudging to purify individuals before ceremonies.

Cathy said, "Tobacco is smoked in the pipe to carry our prayers to the Creator. And when we harvest gifts from Mother Earth or seek knowledge from her creatures, we offer tobacco first. Tobacco is used to give thanks for all we receive." She explained that before you ask an elder for help or teachings, you offer him or her tobacco. I had noticed that the Native women handed Cathy tobacco when they arrived. I thought back to Lynn Andrews putting down tobacco to give thanks for her medicine helpers. Gratitude was already part of my spiritual practice from my twelve-step program, but to be able to make it real through the use of tobacco would make it even more meaningful.

After Cathy finished her teachings, she smudged each of us down with sage, passing the billowing smoke over our entire bodies before we entered the lodge. We crawled in on hands and knees and sat in a circle. The fire keeper brought in the hot stones, one by one, and placed them in the pit as we all said *Boozhoo* (greetings) and *Migwetch* (thank you). These grand-mother and grandfather stones would help us have a good sweat. The door flap was closed, and the lodge became totally dark, hot, and smoky.

I heard a frightened voice say, "It's too hot in here for me, let me out. I'm afraid." A feeling of panic overtook me. *Should I leave?* Cathy calmly opened the flap and invited whoever needed to leave to do so. The two white women exited the lodge but I stayed, trying to calm the disturbing thoughts swirling through my head: *Am I safe? Will I pass out? Am I going to burn to death?* I didn't know how much I could endure, and not knowing was frightening; yet I wanted to face down my fears, so I sat still and prayed.

Soon the ceremony began with drumming, songs, and prayers. The fire keeper brought in more rocks and the heat intensified. With the dense air, it was difficult to breathe. I put my head to the ground, picked up some cedar boughs, and breathed through them. Soon, the songs, drumming, and spirits in the lodge lifted me up, enabling me to submit and endure the discomfort of my body. I had a powerful and deeply moving spiritual experience, seeing the little blue lights of the spirits dancing through the darkness and feeling close to the Creator.

After about two hours, the ceremony ended. We slowly crawled out of the sweat lodge, our bodies limp. Dehydrated, overheated and totally spent, I sprawled on my back on the cool earth, trying to catch my breath. Overhead, a brilliant canopy of stars lit up the evening sky. It was breathtaking! My heart sang out praises to the Creator for the magnificent sight.

After cooling off, we attended to the site, making sure the fire was out and the sacred items – drum, feathers, and medicines – were gathered. As we were cleaning up, Cathy mentioned that a snake had crawled out of the tarp when they unfolded it to build the lodge. A smile crossed my face as I realized the snake, my spirit helper, had been around me once again.

The next day, Cathy introduced me to her husband David, Red Fox, an Ojibwe chief from Wisconsin. David had a strong, distinctive Native American appearance: dark-brown skin, high cheekbones, an aged and scraggly looking face accented by a large, aquiline nose, almond-shaped piercing brown eyes, and long straight white hair. He was a giant of a man but spoke in a gentle and caring manner. Wisdom was etched in his well-worn face and I knew he could deepen my understanding of Native spirituality. Because of my recent experiences, I was anxious to learn more about my spirit helper, so I humbly offered David tobacco, as Cathy had taught, and asked for teachings about snake medicine. He accepted my tobacco and began to talk.

David had a heavy Native American accent and mumbled slightly, so it was difficult to understand what he was saying. I listened intently for about forty-five minutes, picking up only some of his words. *What is he trying to tell me?* I wondered. He ended by comparing a snake to a pinecone. "Like a snake, the pine cone falls to the earth, giving up its life that there may be new life." I was astounded by his words. They were similar to those of my snake, who had also given up its life. *How did he know?*

Later that same day, I ran into the Native vendor I had met at my first powwow in Rapid River. He remembered me and said, "Come here, I have something for you." *He hardly knows me. What can he have for me?* I wondered. He reached inside his tent and pulled out a beautiful wood walking stick with a large brown snake carved around it. He said, "I was traveling out west and saw this and knew it was for you." Overwhelmed and appreciative, I expressed a heartfelt thank-you. Snake medicine was now an integral part of my path.

After the powwow, whenever I'd see a snake I had no fear. I knew that something important was going on in my life and that the snake was there to help me. The snakes became my brothers and sisters, my spirit helpers.

15

Native American Spirituality

I began attending more Native American gatherings and practicing the traditional ways. I also continued to embrace the teachings of my late mentor, Alice, and the spiritual steps of my recovery program. The combination of these three paths provided me with a rich spiritual life. I had found a spirituality that was mine, one that truly resonated with me.

The Native beliefs were simple and grounded: honor the Creator, each other, and all of creation. There was an absence of the multitude of rules that had governed my Catholic religion: such as not eating meat on Friday, fasting before receiving Communion, going to Mass each Sunday, and on and on. In my mind, the rules and laws of the Church were missing the real essence of religion, which is to love God and our neighbor. The rest are superfluous trappings. I found myself becoming more and more disillusioned with organized religions. Recently I saw a bumper sticker that read, "What would Jesus do?" That's a good question. I'm sure He would not choose the law over love or approve of wars being fought in the name of religion.

Although I was no longer a practicing member of the Catholic Church, I did miss the fellowship of my spiritual 'family' of priests, nuns, and teachers – some good, some bad – who kept me in a protective bubble. It was simple and easy; they had the answers and told me what to do, and as long as I followed the rules, I would be loved and taken care of. But now I found myself alone, wandering through life without a compass, facing the onerous task of sorting out my own values and beliefs. I hungered for support, for another spiritual family of like-minded individuals. Thankfully, I found that connectedness within the Native American community, especially with elders like David and Cathy.

David and Cathy welcomed me into their home and became my teachers and friends. David spent many hours talking to me about his customs and spirituality, while my hungry spirit fed on his wisdom. I felt so fortunate to have him as a teacher. Native Americans had plenty of reasons to mistrust white people after their ancestors were lied to, stripped of their land, and forced onto reservations. And while many Natives avoided outsiders, hiding their beliefs and practices, David did not. He freely shared his spirituality with anyone who was sincerely interested. He was a rainbow warrior who taught unity, love, and understanding among all people and was well respected by both Natives and non-Natives.

As I spent more time with David, I saw how fully committed he was to his Native traditional spirituality, yet he was open-minded and knowledgeable about other spiritual paths. We discussed reincarnation, differing cultural prophecies, the use of crystals, astral travel, and the afterlife. I appreciated his openness because I no longer wished to be pigeonholed into one belief system. I wanted to embrace the truth wherever I found it.

David's wife, Cathy, was an outgoing, friendly, caring individual. She was stout, with dark black hair and fair skin, which came from a mixed Indian/White heritage. I liked Cathy from the first moment I met her at the sweat lodge in Baraga. Her native name was Earth Protector, and she had a deep love and respect for what she referred to as 'Mother Earth'. Native Americans were the early environmentalists who were green before it was cool to be green, and Cathy certainly exemplified this. She had a great reverence for the Earth, seeing it as a living entity that needed to be taken care of and protected, for it was the giver of life to all beings.

The Natives teach that we are all related – trees, rocks, water, birds, and creatures – brothers and sisters sharing the same life force energy emanating from the Creator. To honor this connection, tobacco is put down to give thanks before picking a strawberry, gathering medicines or wood, using the water, or taking the life of a rabbit or deer.

I started adopting this practice in my own life by putting tobacco down for whatever I used from the Earth: water, rocks, feathers, trees, vegetables, berries, or sacred medicines. I had empathy for the bushes and trees that endured the heavy weight of snow from UP winter storms. As I skied through the woods, I would knock snow off the branches with my ski poles so they wouldn't break from the weight. I placed leftover food out for the wild animals and camped out and slept on the land. I followed David's admonition not to spit on the ground, for it showed disrespect for our Mother. Slowly, I came to see that the animals, birds, trees, water, and rocks were indeed my brothers and sisters – that we were all in truth related.

Cathy and David had three children: Black Bear, the oldest boy; Dancing Fawn, a girl; and Howling Wolf, the younger boy. They lived in the eastern part of the UP. I'd travel the hundred and fifty miles to their small two-bedroom home for visits. Cathy and David slept in one bedroom, while their three children slept in another. I had to sleep on a single mattress thrown over a handmade wooden frame in a corner of the living room. I had no privacy, but I didn't mind; it was a small price to pay to be around their family. Their simple yet adequate home reflected their meager income, as Cathy was the only breadwinner in the family. David was a respected medicine man and devoted all his time to doctoring, teaching, and conducting sweat lodges and ceremonies.

I spent most of my free time at David and Cathy's house, but one hot, muggy day in August they paid a surprise visit to my home. I was thrilled to see them. That day, as the heat index rose to an uncomfortable 97 degrees, an unusually high temperature for the UP, Cathy and I decided to take a dip in Lake Superior. As we waded out into the cool, refreshing lake, David appeared on the bank and reminded Cathy that she had forgotten to put her tobacco down before entering the water. To Indians, this showed a lack of respect for the spirit of Kitchi-gummi, the Great Water. Cathy and David's exchange left a lasting impression on me, reminding me not to take anything for granted and to always give thanks for the gifts of nature.

Before I learned about the Native American custom of honoring Mother Earth, I used and abused her without a second thought. I'd litter the ground, spit on it, trample down the bushes, and utilize her resources with a feeling of entitlement. I was the master and the Earth was my servant, and I thoughtlessly, selfishly used and took whatever I wanted. Today I am more careful and honor the Earth by recycling, conserving water, putting tobacco down to give thanks before picking berries or swimming in the waters, and respecting our four-legged brothers and sisters.

It is very disturbing to me to see the way our culture abuses and tortures animals in the name of medical research and for clothing, cosmetics, or food. When I started wintering in Arizona in the late nineties, I would make the 2100-mile trip back to Michigan every spring. As I drove through Texas I was appalled at the sight of hundreds of cattle squeezed together in pens, hardly able to move, baking in the blazingly hot sun, waiting to be shipped to the slaughterhouse. My heart ached at the pitiful sight, and it bothered me so much I changed my travel route to avoid seeing these helpless animals.

Later, I learned that after the cattle arrive at the slaughter-house, they are marched single file up a ramp and moved along a conveyor belt where a pneumatic device called a stunner injects a metal bolt about the size of a thick pencil between their eyes, rendering the animals brain dead. Then they're moved along the assembly line, where their chest is ripped open, the aorta pulled out, and they finally bleed to death. Can you imagine the sight, sounds, and smells at these slaughterhouses? These and other practices of animal abuse are in stark contrast to the Native philosophy of respect for all creatures.

Many years ago, I became a vegetarian (except for wild venison), partly due to the unacceptable ways in which we house, feed, and kill the animals that end up on our tables. Add to that the practice of injecting animals with hormones and steroids to increase meat production and the use of cancer-producing additives to preserve the meat. Meat processors add sodium nitrate, which has been linked to colon and gastric cancer, and other substances to make the meat look red and appetizing. If meat was put in the stores without any additives, the color would be an ugly gray consistent with dead flesh. Today I remain a vegetarian because of my health concerns and spiritual beliefs.

The Native American emphasis on the sacredness of the Earth and all its creatures was dear to my heart. I loved being outdoors, soaking in the sights, smells, and sounds of the Creator's handiwork. No longer did I attend church, but I had my cathedral in the woods. When my Catholic mother called on Sundays and tried to guilt-trip me by asking, "Did you go to church today?" I'd respond, "Yes, I took a nice quiet walk in the woods." She didn't like my answer, but that was my truth. I felt closest to God when I was in nature and felt the Creator's presence surrounding me. No wonder I gravitated toward Native American spirituality.

Cathy and David built a sweat lodge behind their house and they invited me to come whenever they had a sweat. They also held spring, fall, and winter ceremonies on their land. David usually conducted the ceremonies, while Cathy led the women's sweat lodges. I was grateful to be able to attend these gatherings, for my heart was hungry as a bear in springtime, wanting to gobble up the spiritual teachings.

The seasonal ceremonies always included a feast to honor the spirit helpers. Everyone brought a dish to share, and before anyone ate David would ask an individual to prepare a plate with a little food from each dish. Then the person would go into the woods to a tree and carefully spoon out the food to symbolically feed the spirit helpers watching over the ceremony. Traditional Natives were forever aware of the presence, help, and protection of the spiritual forces that govern the Universe.

At the ceremonies, elders were served first because Native Americans honor and respect their elders for their wisdom and longevity. Elders are held in high esteem and play a central role in decision making for the tribe, in contrast to modern society, where senior citizens are often disrespected by jokes about aging and senility. Many of our elders are forgotten by their families and hidden away in nursing homes. Rather than embrace the natural beauty of age, we flood the market with products and procedures to produce youthful looks. Cosmetics and plastic surgery are the gods we call upon to keep ourselves looking forever young.

Other Native Americans from across the UP attended the ceremonies at David and Cathy's, and one of them was Sammy, a medicine man. Sammy and his wife Terry were close friends with David and Cathy and visited their home frequently. After I met Sammy, he extended an open invitation to attend sweat lodges at his house in the western UP.

I began alternating between David and Sammy's houses for sweats. I also went up north to the Keweenaw Peninsula for powwows and sweat lodges. I was welcomed and accepted at these Native gatherings, mainly due to my close bond with David and Cathy. I had found a spiritual home among my new Native friends.

David and Cathy had a communal mentality which permeated their interactions with other people. Their emphasis was on others rather than on themselves, and their personal egos were subjugated to the good of the community. At ceremonies and at home, the focus was on serving and taking care of others.

This awareness and love filtered into every aspect of their lives. Being around them and observing their good ways inspired me to be a more loving and giving individual.

Once I went to a powwow with David and Cathy's family and watched their son, Black Bear, who was twelve, dance to every song. I overheard David asking him why he was continually dancing without a rest. Black Bear's response was, "I am dancing for all those who can't dance, who are crippled or who don't have legs." I was amazed at this young boy's level of consciousness, although his actions really shouldn't have surprised me, seeing the great role models surrounding him.

One of the hardest but most important lessons I learned from my interaction with traditional Native Americans was to slow down. They didn't hurry or rush anything and operated on Indian time: things happen when they're supposed to happen. Impatience is one of my greatest faults, and being around Natives gave me the perfect opportunity to learn about the proverbial phrase *Patience is a virtue*. I was forced to slow down, listen, and observe, and in this way I learned. My awareness of myself, others, and the natural world, was enhanced through this process.

Today, I still follow the traditional ways by respecting nature, fasting, vision questing, and attending sweat lodges when possible. I've always had a deep love of nature, and practicing the traditional ways was like coming home to my true religion. I now live in Arizona, far away from the UP, but I hold my own seasonal ceremonies. Four times a year, at the equinox and solstice, I go to isolated places in the forest outside of Sedona, smoke my pipe, and offer up prayers for the people.

One of the places I visit for my ceremonies is an old Indian cliff dwelling. I happened upon it 'by accident' while hiking through the red rocks of Sedona in the Boynton Canyon. I was with my dog Star on a seventy-degree sunny afternoon – a perfect day. As I wandered happily along a small trail, I began to feel sad. I couldn't figure out why I was feeling so downcast. Nothing was bothering me, but the sadness welled up in my heart as tears welled from my eyes. I started sobbing as my dog gazed at me with concern. I had no idea why I was crying.

After I calmed down, I felt drawn to leave the trail and began meandering upward through the rocks. Halfway up the mountain, I gazed toward the summit and saw some stacked rocks and a rough outline of two buildings nestled in a hollow below the peak. Intrigued, I continued my upward climb, and when I reached the hollow I discovered the ruins of an old Indian cliff dwelling. As I turned around, I stood in awe of the magnificent bird's-eye view of Boynton Canyon that lay before me. *How clever of the Indians to hide their dwelling in this elevated, protected, rounded-out piece of the mountain where they could observe the canyon and see anyone approaching,* I thought. I felt as if I was standing on holy ground, so I put some tobacco down to give thanks to the spirits for helping me find this special place.

Just how special these ruins were I would soon find out. Before going to sleep that night, I asked my spirit helpers to give me a dream to explain why I was so sad on the trail. I had a vivid dream about a life as a Hopi Indian. My tribe came through Boynton Canyon and built the cliff dwellings to spend part of the winter. Another tribe, larger than ours, ventured through the canyon, fought us, and we were all killed. I and all my people lost our lives on this land. I had buried my heart in Boynton Canyon. Now, a few times a year, I return to this sacred place and hold ceremony for my people, and remember.

16

Fasting

One weekend while visiting at Cathy and David's, a Native American man and his son from the western UP stopped in, handed David some tobacco, and asked to be put out on a fast. David accepted the man's tobacco and agreed to put them out.

Traditionally, an elder guides a fast by taking individuals to a place in nature and leaving them there for four days, although sometimes it's fewer, then secretly checking up on them each day to see if they're okay.

Although I had attended many sweat lodges and ceremonies, I had never gone into the woods to fast. Maybe it was time to deepen my spiritual walk. I talked to Cathy and she suggested I start with a one-day fast. She told me to go into the woods by my house at sunrise, make a small cedar circle of protection, and sit within it for twenty-four hours.

The circle is a significant symbol in Native American tradition because life and nature is expressed in a circular pattern. In Native beliefs, everything is interconnected and part of the cosmic whole. The circle represents the sun, the moon, the four seasons, and the cycle of life, death, and rebirth. The sun comes forth and goes down in a circle, as does the moon. The birds build their nests in a circle, and the wind at its strongest whirls in a circular manner. Natives built their tepees round like a bird's nest and set them in a circle. They formed talking circles to bring people together in a harmonious way. In the circle, no person was more important than another, and each was allowed to freely speak his or her mind.

The circle or medicine wheel represents the four directions: east, south, west, and north. We all sit in different directions of the wheel at various times of our lives. In one area or period of our life, we might be beginners, sitting in the eastern direction. At other times, we are the wise ones, the teachers, sitting in the northern direction. Rather than viewing spiritual growth from a hierarchical perspective where one moves upward on a ladder, Natives see it as movement around the circle.

The circle is a universal symbol of unity and is inclusive rather than exclusive. One of my favorite epigrams, 'Outwitted', by Edwin Markham, illustrates this unity:

> *He drew a circle that shut me out —*
> *Heretic, a rebel, a thing to flout.*
> *But Love and I had the wit to win:*
> *We drew a circle that took him in!*

At sunrise on a full-moon day in late June, I went into the woods to fast. I made my cedar circle and sat within it, staying there until the next sunrise. I had no water, food, or cigarettes. I'd like to say I had a deep spiritual experience, but I didn't, as my cravings for nicotine, water, and food distracted me. My nicotine withdrawal was intense, and I kept wishing I had a cigarette. After a few hours, I became very thirsty and hungry. It's hard to focus on the spiritual when the body is screaming to be taken care of. I'm sure I'd be the weakest link on the TV show *Survivor*. For twenty-four hours, however, I *did* outlast my body's cravings, but it certainly was a struggle.

The highlight of the evening was a flurry of animal activity. As the full moon cast its soft glow over the land, animals began dancing in the moonlight. Wide-eyed squirrels and chipmunks darted into my circle, curious, checking me out. I sat very still, observing them, amazed at how close they came. Not far away, I heard the snapping of branches and crunching of underbrush as larger animals – probably deer, bear and coyote – prowled through the woods. I wasn't afraid – I felt safe in my cedar circle – but I was astounded by how alive the woods became at night, a hidden wonder unfolding in my presence. It reminded me of my first scuba dive, when I was amazed by the wondrous life that existed underwater.

I went on my second fast a few years later. Joe, a Marquette Native American elder, led me up Eagle Mountain, named for the rock formation shaped like an eagle lying at the base of the mountain. At the top, there was an expansive view of Lake Superior to the east and dense woods in the other directions. I used cedar boughs to form my circle and tied yellow, red, black, and white ribbons to sticks, placing them around the circle in the four directions, starting in the east.

My intent in fasting was to purify my body, commune with nature, and be open to messages from the spirit world. Unlike my first fast, I quickly moved through my physical discomfort. After I transcended my body, I found myself vibrating on a different plane. Absorbed in a contemplation of nature, I observed the birds and listened to their varied calls, watched the tiny insects traverse the rocks, and gazed out over the lake and land. Hours went by without an awareness of time. I existed in a deeply relaxed meditative state.

On the mountaintop, I became acutely aware of my oneness with the Creator and all of creation. The trees, wind, sun, moon, birds, animals, water, and rocks were my brothers and sisters. I became aware of my need to respect them and live in harmony with them. I received teachings from the spirits about the significance of the four directions, the medicines on the earth, and our animal helpers. After two days, I came down from the mountain with a renewed spirit and a grateful heart.

From time to time, I'd go on minifasts from sunrise to sunset. Often before going into an evening sweat lodge, I would fast for the day. One time when I was out on a minifast, I heard this small voice inside whisper that my spirit name was Moon Woman. I knew that Native Americans had spirit names given to them by an elder, but I never expected to receive one on my own. I was confused, so afterward I went to see my teacher David and told him what had happened. He proceeded to give me some teaching about spirit names.

David said, "A spirit name is an animal, object, or phrase that personifies the energy of the individual. Our English names of Jane, John, Mary, or Joe are not really descriptive of who we are in the eyes of the Creator. Think about a young boy who is a fast runner. His spirit name might be Running Deer. Or a girl who is always laughing and jovial might be Laughing Maiden. Moon Woman is *your* spirit name, and you also have a clan that goes with it. Your clan is Eagle Clan. So when you speak to the Creator, use your spirit name, Moon Woman, and your clan name." Ever since that day, I follow this practice in my prayers to the Creator.

Hunting

While I was visiting at Sammy's house one day, David showed up. Although it was nine o'clock at night and dark outside, David said he and Sammy were going deer hunting, and he invited me to come along. I wondered how he was going to shoot a deer in the dark, but I accepted his invitation. Before leaving, David placed some tobacco on the ground by a cedar tree to give thanks and to call in the spirit of the deer who was to come to him.

I squeezed between the two men in the front seat of Sammy's old beat-up truck, filled with anticipation. I had never been deer hunting and didn't have the slightest idea what we were going to do. After we'd been riding awhile, Sammy turned onto a remote dirt road, slowed down, and came to a stop. Quietly, David got out of the truck, leaving the door ajar. He slowly raised his rifle to his shoulder and then motioned with his head to Sammy. Sammy turned on the truck's spotlight and shined it down into a deep ravine. To my amazement, there stood a herd of seven or eight deer frozen in the traditional 'deer in the headlight' stance. David aimed and fired, instantly felling a large buck, as the other deer jumped and scattered. *Leave it to the clever Indians,* I thought, *to figure out the easiest way to get a deer.*

Quickly, Sammy and David retrieved the deer and placed it in the back of the truck, because nighttime hunting was illegal. Sammy floored the gas and we escaped with our forbidden prey. After we got home, they gutted the deer, butchered it, and had their meat for the coming months. Both David and Sammy's families depended upon venison for their winter food.

UP residents love to hunt. Almost everyone in the UP, men and women alike, seem to become afflicted with 'deer fever' around November 15th. Teenagers skip school, businesses shut down, and police are on skeleton crews as masses head to the woods to hunt. Business is forgotten. Hunting season is like an extended national holiday. No one is around town during deer season, which lasts from November 15th to the 30th. The woods are replete with people in massive hypnotic trances seeking one thing: to bring home a treasured trophy.

In 1989, I caught deer fever and had a yearning to hunt. I enjoyed living isolated in the woods and thought someday I might move further away from civilization, relocating to Alaska or the Northwest Territory. I wondered if I'd be able to sustain myself by living off the land. To do that, I needed to learn how to hunt. I thought if I could hunt in a good way, by putting tobacco down and calling in the spirit of a deer, as I had seen David do, it would be all right. I'd eat the venison and honor other parts of the deer by keeping the antlers and tanning the hide.

I bought a 12-gauge shotgun and practiced firing. I felt like Annie Oakley when I had it in my hands. Having had my power stripped from me as an abused child, it was empowering to be able to handle and fire a big shotgun. I felt strong and in control, feelings that were unfamiliar to me. Later I discovered that a 12-gauge shotgun is not the best type of gun to use for deer hunting. The seasoned hunters in the UP mostly used 30-30 or 30.06 rifles, but I was a novice and didn't know any better.

I went to the woods and found a spot on a ridge overlooking a small valley. I put tobacco on the ground and started building my blind. I gathered fallen branches and stacked them on top of one another, making a three-sided enclosure, leaving the northern direction open for entrance. Inside the blind, I poked an opening through the branches where I could position my shotgun.

For two weeks before opening day I placed apples in a bait pile about forty yards from my blind in the western direction along the ridge. In this strategic location, I could sit in my blind and face downwind of the bait pile to cover my scent. The day before opening day I aired my brightly colored blaze-orange hunting clothes – jacket, pants, hat and gloves – outside in the fresh air. Then I broke several branches off a cedar tree (putting tobacco down first) and rubbed the foliage all over my clothes to disguise the human scent.

Before daybreak on November 15th, I headed to the woods with a flashlight and shotgun. With stealthy footsteps I traversed the winding, woodland trail to my blind. Sitting quietly in my blind, I waited until daybreak, when the rising sun lit up the morning sky. It was so peaceful sitting there surrounded by the sounds of nature: the call of the birds, the sharp, metallic chirping sound of the squirrels, and the rustling of the wind through the trees. I watched the chipmunks scurrying along the ground and saw the high-flying squirrels leaping from one pine tree to another. *No wonder so many people head to the woods during deer season. It's not just about hunting, but basking in the solitude and wonders of nature.* After five or six hours of sitting without seeing a deer, I took a break and went home for lunch.

I returned in mid-afternoon and waited. Darkness began to fall and I was about to leave the blind. Then seemingly out of nowhere a four-point buck appeared and headed for my bait pile. I fought to control my nerves as I slowly raised my shotgun and aimed. Bam! I hit it, and it went down. To my horror, I watched as it struggled to get up but couldn't because I had shot it in the hip and paralyzed its back legs. I sat frozen, not knowing what to do, my heart breaking as I watched the deer frantically trying to stand up. Then, as if someone had slapped me in the face and screamed, 'Do something!', I pulled out of my immobile state. I had to end the suffering. I jumped out of my blind, approached the deer, aimed, and shot straight through its heart.

Adrenaline was coursing so strongly through my body I thought I was going to have a heart attack. Electrifying energy surged through me, as if I had just touched a live wire, leaving me shaken. An exhilarating feeling of success arose, intermingled with sadness over seeing the dead deer lying on the ground. I couldn't believe I had actually killed a deer. It was getting dark and I had to get it out of the woods, but I couldn't do it on my own. It was too heavy. Not expecting to actually bag a deer, I had no game plan as to what to do next.

I thought about my friends, Jeff and Katrina, who lived nearby. I ran breathlessly down the path to my car and drove quickly to their house. Jeff accompanied me back to the woods, where he tied a rope around the buck's two hind legs and dragged it out of the forest. After we got back to his house, Jeff skinned and gutted the deer as I watched, sickened by the gruesome sight and fighting the urge to throw up. I thanked God for Jeff's being available and willing to help me, for I never could have handled skinning and gutting a deer. I imagine some hunters would argue that if I was unwilling to do the dirty work, I shouldn't hunt. They might be right. After Jeff finished, he tied one end of a rope around the buck's neck and tossed the other end over a tree branch to hoist the deer up into the air for the evening.

The next morning, Jeff, Katrina, and I faced the arduous task of butchering the deer. We spent hours cutting the venison into steaks and grinding the rest into burgers. Now we had our winter meat. The antlers I saved, and I sent the hide away to be tanned, knowing I could make pouches and clothing from the leather. All that winter I enjoyed the delicious venison, and with every meal I gave thanks to the spirit of that deer who had sacrificed its life that I might eat.

The following year I decided to go deer hunting once again. This time, I bought a more powerful 30-30 rifle, hoping to fell the deer with one shot, having learned my lesson from the previous year. I went back to my spot in the woods and rebuilt my blind in the same location; but instead of placing the bait pile to the west on the ridge, I put it eighty yards below me in the valley.

Again, the first day of deer season, right at dusk, an eight-point buck approached the bait pile. Nervously, I looked through my scope, aimed, and fired. The deer jumped straight up in the air about three feet and ran off. I couldn't believe I had missed it. I decided to go down and check the area, and with freshly fallen snow on the ground, it was easy to spot some blood droppings. My heart dropped. I had hit the buck, and now it was running through the woods wounded. I had to find it. I couldn't let it suffer.

Following the blood drops through the snow, I came onto an old logging road and ran into Tom and Sarah, neighbors who were also hunting. They offered to help track the deer, and we traced the droppings about two hundred more yards until we found the buck lying dead on the side of a hill. My heart was heavy, seeing the beautiful animal lying there and thinking about its struggle to survive. But there was no time for tears; it was getting dark and we had to get the deer out of the woods. We hauled the buck to Tom and Sarah's nearby truck and then I hiked to mine to follow them to their house. When I arrived, Tom had already started gutting the deer. Once again, we had venison for the winter.

This time, however, things were different. I started having nightmares about the deer suffering, disturbing visions of that gentle creature fighting so hard to survive and running bleeding and wounded through the woods before giving up its courageous struggle. These images also haunted my waking hours. The killing ripped my soul open to a new spiritual level. My connection to all of God's creatures could not be reconciled with taking one of their lives. It would be different if I needed the meat to survive, but I didn't. I don't judge others who hunt for food, and I think it is more humane than our slaughterhouse practices, but *my* hunting days were over.

A week later, on Thanksgiving Day, I drove to Munising with my dog Star to spend the day with Sandi and her family. I had met Sandi at Alice's house a few years earlier, and we had quickly become friends. Sandi, her two girls, and I had a lovely dinner and lively conversation. I drove home about 9pm, turned on the outside flood light, and let Star hang out in the yard for a while. All was quiet. My night-owl energy kicked in and I stayed up until four in the morning painting designs on sweatshirts for Christmas presents for my family.

When I awoke around noon, I put on some water for tea, opened the refrigerator, grabbed a bundle of fresh parsley from my garden, and started cutting it up to freeze for the winter. Star whined to go outside so I opened the door to let her out and immediately she began barking wildly on the porch. I looked outside and saw nothing unusual, figuring she saw or smelled an animal in the woods. I brought her inside and told her to be quiet, but she insisted on going back out. She stood rigid on the porch barking incessantly, desperately trying to alert me, but I was oblivious to any danger as I continued cutting up the parsley.

Suddenly her barking increased by a few decibels, and as I looked up I saw a man running through my yard toward the house. My first thought was there had been an accident on the highway and someone was coming for help. As I walked around my kitchen counter toward the front door, the man burst through the unlocked door with Star nipping at his leg. Kicking at Star, he shouted at me, "Give me your money!".

I saw a long hunting knife in his hand and stood frozen, unable to take in the reality of what was going on, as he continued shouting, "Give me your money. Give me your money". Finally it sank in. *I'm being robbed.* This was the last thing I'd expected to happen in the UP, where crime was almost unknown. Neighbors left their doors unlocked and keys in the car in case someone might need help. It was a friendly, trusting rural environment.

Since I seldom had cash on me, I knew I was in trouble. I ran for the door to the upstairs bedroom and almost had it slammed shut when he jerked it open. We stood face to face, only a couple of feet apart. His navy blue ski cap was pulled down to the top of his wild and crazy-looking eyes. *Is he drugged up?* I couldn't tell. His face was rough and unshaven with days-old stubble, making him look even more menacing. Standing over six feet tall with a stocky build, he could easily overpower, rape, or kill me. My body trembled as scenes from the movie *Psycho* flashed through my mind.

Suddenly, he took a step back with a bewildered look and stared down at my right hand, which was still holding the butcher knife I had been cutting the parsley with. I was so flustered I hadn't realized it was in my hand. Seeing it gave me a little leverage, and I said, "Take it easy. I'll give you what I have." With my left hand I reached for my purse sitting on the nearby table, pulled out eight dollars, and handed it to him. It was all I had.

"Give me *all* your money," he screamed. I started crying because I didn't have any more money in the house.

"I don't have anymore," I said. "I never carry cash."

He glared at me with a threatening yet puzzled look, like he was trying to decide what to do. At this point, Star moved up behind him. Distracted by her movement, he turned to look and immediately I made my escape, bolting to the bathroom and slamming and locking the door. I was safe, but trapped in my self-imposed prison. I looked out the window and saw him walk into my outdoor sauna, come out with a bedroll over his shoulder, and stroll leisurely down my driveway as if he were going to Sunday church.

I ran to my bedroom phone. The line was dead. I ran down to the other phone in the kitchen. Dead. I was stranded in the house as he was getting away. Then I heard a sound. Turning around, I saw two women on the shore in the front of my cabin playing with their dog. Knocking hard on the window, I motioned for them to come around to the front door, where I related what had happened. We ran together to the neighbor's house to call the police. The Chocolay Township police were there too soon for the robber to have had time to walk or run to the main highway. Evidently, he was hiding in the woods somewhere.

The police discovered he had spent time in my sauna, where they found cigarette butts on the floor and apple cores from the stored deer bait. He had also rifled through the glove compartment of my car, undoubtedly looking for money, and had cut my phone line on the porch. The police brought in a tracking dog that picked up his scent in the sauna and followed it about a half mile into the woods. Then the trail wound back over our road, and that's where the dog lost his scent.

The officer asked if I would be willing to give a description to the state police sketch artist. I agreed, not knowing that we had to drive a hundred miles to Iron Mountain to find him at deer camp. The police officer zipped down the snow-covered road at a rate that gave me trouble remembering my own name by the time we'd reached the camp. I gave the best description I could and the police ran a sketch in the paper the next day, but the man was never caught.

Prior to the robbery, I had no curtains on my windows and never locked my door. The robber only got eight dollars from me, but he took much more. He stole my peace of mind. I hung up heavy curtains and secured the front door with a bolt lock. I was afraid to go out after dark even with my dog. The robber knew where I lived and he knew I was alone. He could come back. I kept my rifle out where I could easily reach it. I guess the adage 'what comes around goes around' is true. Maybe it was karma! Just a week before, I had killed my second deer. Now *I* had become the stalked prey. It took over a year before I felt any sense of safety in my own home.

18

The Fifth Step

When I had finished the first four steps of my recovery program, I was ready to tackle the difficult fifth step: admitting to God, to myself, and to another human being the exact nature of my wrongs. I had no trouble admitting to God and myself my misdeeds, but my fragile ego balked at the idea of revealing my darkest secrets to another person. *What would that person think of me?* For so many years I had worked hard to look good and say the right things; the opinion of others was very important to me. Now I had to get real, eat crow, and humble myself by admitting all my wrongs to another person.

The most difficult part would be talking about my promiscuous sex and sleeping with married men. And my biggest stumbling block and the thing I felt most ashamed of was my molestation of the child I had babysat when I was twelve years old. I was so ashamed of this deed I felt I would rather die than tell someone, but I knew if I was going to do a thorough fifth step, I had to include it. As I noted earlier, there is a saying that you're only as sick as your secrets, and this secret was killing me.

My sponsor, Mary, suggested I find someone I trusted to hear my fifth step. Since my spirituality was centered on Native American teachings, I decided to ask Sammy, the medicine man, who was familiar with twelve-step work. Sammy agreed and suggested we do it in a sweat lodge, which I thought was a great idea. In the total darkness of the lodge, which reminded me of the blackened confessional box, I nervously poured out my past failings: sleeping with married men, lying, promiscuous sex, drinking and smoking too much pot, selfishness, and the molestation.

When I finished, I took a deep breath and nervously waited

for Sammy's reprimand, but one never came. Instead, he surprised me by asking, "Do you want to go traveling?" I wasn't exactly sure what he meant by traveling, but I suspected it involved an out-of-body experience. Afraid but curious, I hesitantly said yes, not knowing what to expect.

Sammy started rhythmically banging on his drum while telling me to imagine myself falling backward into the darkness. To do this was a leap of faith; I had to let go. As I did, I started tumbling backward very rapidly into the darkness. At first I felt out of control and frightened, but those feelings passed when I found myself floating outside the lodge and looking down on it. It didn't occur to me that being outside of my body traveling was unusual, for I was totally present and immersed in my experience.

Slowly I started to rise up, and I could see the yard, the neighborhood, and the nearby city. I was awestruck as I continued to rise, seeing the state of Michigan, then the United States, and finally the entire earth. Finally, I was propelled into outer space and saw planets, stars, and various galaxies spinning.

As I traveled through space, a tiny white light appeared in the distance. It grew brighter as it approached me. Soon the light engulfed me and I sensed a loving and peaceful Presence enveloping me. My whole body tingled as I relaxed in this Presence, feeling serene and content. No words were exchanged; we were conversing on a nonverbal plane. The most poignant communication was emotional, as I felt an all-encompassing, overpowering love passing back and forth between us. I don't know how long I stayed in the light, but I do know that I didn't want to leave and let go of the beautiful, soulful feeling I was experiencing.

Eventually, way off in the distance, I heard someone whispering my name: "Elaine, Elaine, Elaine." The voice of the medicine man was calling me back to the lodge. I came back into my body very slowly, like someone awakening from a deep sleep.

Everything felt surreal. The heaviness of my body was oppressive compared to the lightness I had just experienced. I felt intense disappointment at being back in the density of the physical.

Sammy's voice jolted me out of my altered state. He said, "I was worried about you and had a hard time bringing you back. You were gone for a long time." He added, "A person can cross over to the other side while traveling. The soul which is out of the body can stay in the spirit world and drop the body." I nodded, fully understanding why a person would want to do that.

Traveling in the sweat lodge was not my first out-of-body experience. The first time my spirit left my body was when I was in the convent, meditating on my bed, and found myself floating up on the ceiling looking down on myself. Then, when I was fasting, my spirit was out of my body for long periods of time. Since then, when meditating, I often find myself in an out-of-body or altered state of consciousness.

Not until I read Cara Stiles' study, 'The Influence of Childhood Dissociative States from Sexual Abuse on the Adult Woman's Spiritual Development', did I get a clearer understanding of why it was easy for me to leave my body.

As I've mentioned previously, dissociation is the ability to mentally detach from the reality of the abuse by going away, floating outside the body. Stiles' study found that women survivors of childhood sexual abuse can use their dissociative skills to experience altered states of consciousness in an intentional manner, as through meditation, rather than as a childhood defense mechanism to escape trauma. She states, "It would appear that once these women [in the study] were exposed to other states of consciousness, despite the fact that their first exposure was the consequence of a traumatic ordeal, they then had the proclivity to reenter those states."[6] Once a person has an out-of-body experience during trauma, once that state is known, they can return to altered states of consciousness.

Some women mentioned that the place they dissociated to as a child was so pleasant and provided so much comfort that they had an unconscious yearning to return to that place. I believe this was one of the reasons why I smoked marijuana. I was trying to induce a return to a place of altered consciousness. Later, I discovered that I didn't need drugs to do that and could reach these altered states through meditation, fasting, and sweat lodge experiences.

Stiles' study also supported the hypothesis that dissociative states experienced during childhood sexual abuse influenced the adult woman's spiritual development. There was a search for purpose and meaning in these women's lives, and they all developed a strong spiritual belief system. Some of the women alluded to their sexual abuse and dissociation as the motivating force behind their career choices.

I can surely relate to this, for after my sexual abuse I decided to become a psychologist and help others. I also started asking existential questions: *Who am I? What is my purpose? What's it all about?* I then engaged in a search for meaning through various nontraditional spiritual paths.

Stiles also mentions clinician Norah M. Sargent's study of the effects of childhood abuse on adult spirituality. Stiles says, "She [Sargent] found that many adult survivors left the traditional religious domain where God is personified and instead related to God best as a nonpersonified image. She uses the example of God as nature."[7] I could easily relate to this idea, for it is within nature that I so easily find God. My Native American beliefs taught me to respect the Creator and all of creation.

19

Closure

Adult survivors of childhood sexual abuse sometimes need a comforting or satisfying sense of finality, a closure, to complete their healing. Some survivors will seek closure, while others won't. Closure can come in many forms, and no one way is right for everyone. For some, closure might involve confronting the perpetrator or pressing criminal charges against him. Since some women do not recall the abuse until later in life; their abuser might be dead, or the statute of limitations might have passed so they are unable to press charges.

Going into therapy and working through the abuse and its consequences is another way to obtain closure. Some women may just need to break the silence and tell a loved one their unspeakable secret, while others find comfort by joining a victims' support group. Getting involved in social activism focused on preventing child sexual abuse or writing about it can provide closure.

For me, my anger toward my abusers had subsided through therapy, but something felt unfinished. The missing piece emerged one day while I was meditating. I needed to confront my abuser. The thought entered my mind and replayed over and over that I needed to talk to Ronnie, my brother's childhood friend who had pretended to be mine. My father, the abusive bosses, and the priests were all deceased, but Ronnie was still living. I could face up to him, but to do it would require a lot of courage.

I froze in horror every time I thought about calling him. *How would he respond? Would he deny everything and blame me?* In my perfect world, I needed him to take responsibility for his actions so I could quit blaming myself. However, talking to him could go either way, making things worse or better. *Could my heart handle a rejection or a denial from him?*

For two months I agonized over my dilemma, thinking about what I needed to say and rehearsing it over and over. I wanted to come from a centered place and be direct but gentle, and since I had released a lot of my anger in therapy, I thought I could do this. What I really wanted was for Ronnie to admit it was his fault and say he was sorry. If I didn't get that, I'd still be okay; but surely if he owned his part, more healing and closure could follow.

One day when I was tired of stressing over the whole situation, I decided to call him. I found his telephone number in the white pages and, with my stomach churning, dialed his number. I read right from my prepared script:

"Hello, Ronnie, this is Elaine Hodge. Do you have a few minutes to talk?" Of course he was surprised to hear from me, for it had been over fifty years since we had last spoken.

"Yes, I can talk," he said in a nervous voice.

I went right into my rehearsed words. "Ronnie, I need to let you know that because you sexually abused me as a child, I have struggled with intimacy and relationship issues throughout my life. You were not my only abuser, so I don't put all the blame on you, but your actions certainly had a negative impact on me."

"I was praying this day would never come," Ronnie replied. "I tried to forget all about this, and was hoping we would never talk about it. I've felt so guilty over the years, and I'm so sorry for what I did."

His response left me breathless. I heard those freeing words I had needed to hear. He took responsibility for the abuse and apologized. But then he did an about-face, trying to justify his actions.

"I was going through a rough time, and I think it was just adolescent behavior. We were only a couple of years apart in age." I didn't let him wiggle off the hook.

"Ronnie, you were five years older than me. I was nine when it began, and you were fourteen. You continued to abuse me until you were seventeen." Again, he apologized.

"What I did wasn't right. I am truly sorry for having hurt you." I thanked him for his apology and said, "I forgive you. Maybe this can be a healing for both of us. I hope so."

With that, I said goodbye and wished him well. I hung up the phone with tears trickling down my cheeks, overwhelmed by my emotions. All the anticipation, all the worry, was now over, and I felt so relieved. As hard as it was to make, this call closed a painful chapter from my past.

All that is necessary for evil to succeed is that good men do nothing.
Edmund Burke

A couple of months after my conversation with Ronnie, I suspected a nearby neighbor might be sexually abusing his grandchild. Another neighbor told me this man had inappropriately touched her seven-year-old, and she would not allow her daughter to be around him anymore. My concern was for his eight-year-old granddaughter, who spent a fair amount of time at his home. Once I heard him tell his grandchild to reach in his pocket for some change, and she did. Other times he would hold her on his lap and constantly fondle her as she sat there looking very uncomfortable. Bells and whistles were going off in my head as my concern for this young girl increased.

I tried to ignore the situation, telling myself it was none of my business, but an uncomfortable feeling gnawed at me. *Something is going on!* I thought about my own abuse and how I wished someone had done something to help me. I had to try and protect this child. If nothing was going on, then so be it, but if abusive behavior was occurring, then someone needed to know.

After much deliberation, I called Child Protective Services and told them about this man's history and what I had observed with his granddaughter. I felt deeply relieved when they said they would investigate the case, assuring me my call would remain confidential. I thanked them and hung up. I never found out the results of the investigation, but I had the satisfaction of knowing I tried to help.

Recently, another situation surfaced that demanded my attention. A friend of mine who is a computer technician told me he was fixing a man's computer and found child pornography on it. I knew the man he was talking about. The news sickened me, especially when he told me he felt like throwing up after seeing some of the explicit pictures. I felt my blood pressure soar, my chest tighten, and anger well up inside me. I couldn't stand the thought of this fifty-five year old man seeking sexual gratification through graphic and exploitative pictures of children.

I said to my friend, "We have to do something about this. It's a crime and needs to be reported." With a typical 'duck your head in the sand' mentality, he replied, "I don't want to get involved." I thought, *Isn't this the way most individuals react? That's why people get by with these things.* My conscience bothered me, however, and I couldn't ignore it. The need to do the right thing and my own childhood abuse prompted me to call the police and report this man. I don't know what happened because I was not privy to the results of their investigation.

It baffled me as to why so many sexual situations were coming to my attention, but I knew I could no longer stand quietly by and allow injustice to prevail. Without being asked, I was becoming an advocate for child protection.

20

Staying Awake

My post-abuse journey to find meaning for my life took many twists and turns, going round and round, up and down, but it always wound back to me, to my accountability, to my willingness to walk with higher principles and be of service to others. The teaching of some contemporary spiritual teachers to 'wake up' and stay aware of our true Self has helped me over the past couple of years.

There is a saying, 'Once you wake up, you can't go back to sleep, but you can doze a little'. My spiritual aim is to wake up, stay awake, and continually raise my consciousness from an egocentric pattern of living to a higher level of development in which I know and live my true spiritual nature. Not an easy task! The Armenian-Greek teacher of the Fourth Way, G. I. Gurdjieff, asserted that man lives most of his life in a hypnotic, sleeping state and needs to wake up so he can participate in the Work of God. Gurdjieff used the word 'Work' with a capital W to refer to the personal work on self to raise consciousness.

E. J. Gold, a contemporary spiritual teacher, also emphasizes the need for man to wake up, to not get lulled into what he refers to as the mechanistic operations of the body/mind machine. I joined a spiritual study group focusing on E. J. Gold's book *Practical Work on Self.* Each week we read a new chapter, went over its meaning, and then set the intention to work the recommended exercise in the following week. All the exercises were geared toward awakening the body/mind machine so that it can be used as a transformational apparatus for the evolution of the Being, the essential Self, the Soul.

Work on self is never easy and takes a commitment to practice, practice, practice; to live in the moment and observe how the mind and emotions operate; to ask, *Who is really in charge of my life? My spirit or Higher Self, or my mind and emotions?*

How easy it is to identify with our emotions. Every day we hear people make statements such as "I'm depressed", "I'm angry", "I'm so disappointed", or "I'm hurt". Who is the 'I' in these statements? Would it not be more accurate to say the mind had a thought, drew a conclusion, and experienced an emotion? Although we *have* a body, a mind, and emotions, that is not who we *are*. We are spiritual beings experiencing an incarnation in a body/mind machine. When we identify with just the body, intellect, and emotions, we limit ourselves.

Red Hawk, a spiritual seeker, has written a small but powerful book called *Self Observation*, in which he talks about the importance of observing one's thoughts and emotions in order to awaken. Self observation is the key to good spiritual practice, for it enables one to realize the ancient spiritual teaching 'know thyself'. Red Hawk stresses the need to observe without judging, because judgment leads to greater identification with that which is observed.

I understand this concept because in the past I'd work hard on trying to get rid of my undesirable character defects only to find myself more entangled in them. As I focused on my defects, I judged myself harshly and identified with those negative traits. *I am a bad person, too controlling, judgmental, and angry.* The list went on. But as I learned to let go of self-judgment and merely observe my thoughts while bringing my focus back to my body and breathing, I could let the thoughts just pass through and not be that important. This helped me detach from the constant obsessive chattering of my active mind.

I have heard it said that we have over seventy-thousand thoughts each day, and many of these are repeated thoughts. Part of the mind's job is to analyze, dissect, and judge: *this is good, this is bad; I like this, I don't like that.* I can let these seventy-thousand thoughts come and go without giving them power over me.

Usually, my thoughts precede my emotions, so if I don't give thoughts free rent in my head, if I don't obsess, I can reduce my emotional reactions. I notice that as I simply observe my thoughts, without judgment, my mind is quieted and the frequency of thoughts diminishes. This is in alignment with the Heisenberg Principle: the law that tells us that the act of observation alters that which is being observed.

Sadly, few people are interested in waking up, and choose to live their lives in quiet desperation, content with their daily routines, material pursuits, and petty satisfactions: to run to sales at Walmart or Penney's; to watch football on weekends; to get a new car or wide-screen TV; to see their children receive good grades; or to dream of winning the big lottery. They come into the world asleep and leave asleep, missing out on the true meaning of life unless someone shows them a different way. Unless they become dissatisfied with their ordinary lives, they will not search for a spiritual teacher or school or read spiritual books or be concerned for matters of the soul.

But for those who are serious about waking up, there are many ways to raise one's consciousness. Some use the path of knowledge, involving reading and studying spiritual works, while others find a spiritual teacher. Meditation can raise our awareness level, as can practicing good works. Inquiry, or asking existential questions such as *Who am I? What is my purpose? Why am I here?* can also be helpful on the spiritual journey.

Various teachers over the years have challenged their students to grow by posing such questions. Gurdjieff encouraged his students to ask, 'What is my chief weakness?' in order to look at that which interferes with the Work we are called to do. Often, our chief weakness is hidden, and we need someone outside ourselves – a teacher – to help us identify it, but once we are aware of our chief weakness, it loses its power to interfere with the Work. My teacher Alice asked me to go inward and reflect on the question 'Who am I?' in order to find my true nature.

In his book *Feast or Famine: Teachings on Mind and Emotions*, Lee Lozowick, another contemporary teacher, recommends asking the question 'Who am I kidding?' or 'Who is it that is under illusion?'. He emphasizes the need to tame or train the mind through enquiry, meditation, self-observation, and rubbing up against phrases like 'Draw no conclusions mind'. If you observe the mind, you will see that it is constantly drawing conclusions, and those conclusions can lead to judgment and emotional reaction.

Recently, a good friend and I were talking on the phone when she abruptly, and in my mind rudely, cut me off with a biting comment. Immediately, my mind started playing with the scenario: *I must have said something to upset her. She really doesn't like me. She's a mean and untrustworthy person* – and on and on. These thoughts evolved into hurt feelings on my part. I have to ask myself what would have happened if I had stayed in a 'draw no conclusion' state of mind. After all, I really didn't know what was going on with her, and there was an array of possible explanations. Maybe she was having a bad day – was tired, hungry, or busy. By drawing a conclusion and personalizing the situation, I made a judgment, took a stand, and separated myself from her.

I am a work in progress, but maybe that's okay. One of my twelve-step sayings is 'progress not perfection'. Every day, I work on observing myself without judging – staying present and being available to serve those who come into my life. Most days I'm successful, but other days...oh well, it's 'progress, not perfection'.

Epilogue

Today, I have a sense of peace and wellbeing I never imagined. I have learned how to accept life on life's terms – to not fight what life throws at me, but rather to turn it into a positive learning experience. I have been able to forgive those who have harmed me, to accept their humanness and realize we are all fragile beings trying to do the best we can. Does this mean that sexual or any other kind of abuse is alright? Absolutely not! It is a crime that tears the fibers of one's soul, destroying a healthy sense of self. But it gives both the abuser and the abused a chance to come together – as Ronnie and I did – to forgive and to heal.

So many positive changes have occurred in my life. Today the howling of the neighbor's neglected dog no longer throws me into an emotional tailspin as it used to. When I hear Buddy howl, I visualize myself giving him a big hug and mentally send him some loving energy. Sometimes, when the neighbor isn't home, I go next door and pet him through the fence, talk to him, and give him a little treat. No longer do I feel like I want to kill my neighbor and steal his dog. I notice that the anger I carried for so many years toward my abusers and others has dissipated. I find myself able to be more loving toward family and friends. This is the person I am meant to be!

Ever since I can remember, I have wanted to be of service to others. Today, I realize the way I can be of greatest service is to work on myself – to stay awake and observe my thoughts and emotions. Being awake is another way of saying that I am in tune with my spiritual self and operating from that sacred space. From that space, true service naturally occurs, and it is not service that originates in the ego with a do-goodism or savior mentality. From that space, one inherently knows how to serve to further God's work. Every morning I affirm this intention: 'May everything I do this day be for the glory of God and the benefit of all Beings everywhere!'

Over the years, I have finally come to a clear understanding that happiness is an inside job. It's not 'out there' somewhere. It's not about finding someone or something to fill the void. For many years I told myself I could only be happy if I met the right man. So far, he hasn't appeared, but I am still very happy. I'm content with my life and feel fulfilled in my work. Spirit, my dog, and River, Gracie and Migese, my three cats, are my loving companions. Years of recovery meetings, therapy, and my spiritual journey have brought me to this place of peace.

Endnotes

1. http://www.rainn.org/statistics.

2. *American Journal on Addictions* 6:273-283.

3. Cara L. Stiles, 'The Influence of Childhood Dissociative States from Sexual Abuse on the Adult Woman's Spiritual Development', *Journal of Heart Centered Therapies* 10 (2007): 9-63.

4. http://www.ncjrs.gov/pdffiles/1/nij/210346.pdf,2006.

5. http://www.everydayhealth.com/sexual-health/dr-laura-berman-childhood-abuse-and-adult-relationships.

6. Stiles, 'The Influence of Childhood Dissociative States from Sexual Abuse on the Adult Woman's Spiritual Development', *Journal of Heart Centered Therapies* 10 (2007): 48.

7. Ibid., 41.

Bibliography

Andrews, Lynn. *Medicine Woman*. New York: Tarcher, 2006.

Gold, E. J. *Practical Work on Self*. Nevada City, CA: Gateways/IDHHB, 1992.

Lozowick, Lee. *Feast or Famine: Teachings on Mind and Emotions*. Prescott, AZ: Hohm Press, 2008.

Norwood, Robin. *Women Who Love Too Much: When You Keep Wishing and Hoping He'll Change*, reprint ed. Gallery Books, 2008.

Red Hawk, *Self Observation*. Prescott, AZ: Hohm Press, 2009.

Acknowledgments

I extend my deepest gratitude

    To my mother, who instilled in me a deep belief in God.

    To Alice, my first spiritual teacher, who opened my eyes to a new way of seeing reality and showered me with unconditional love.

    To Red Fox, my wise Native American teacher, and all Native elders who embraced me on the Red Road.

    To my father and all my abusers, who gave me the opportunity to learn forgiveness and propelled me onto a spiritual journey.

    To my sisters, brothers, sisters-in-law and brothers-in-law, who have supported and accompanied me throughout my life.

    To Bara Rogers, my mentor, advisor and friend, who believed in me and in this book.

    To Nancy Lewis, my coach, editor and spiritual friend, whose wisdom and guidance helped make this book possible.

    To Cheri, my dear friend, who provided assistance through her vast technological knowledge.

    To Caron Goode, Ed.D., my first editor and spiritual sister.

    To Nicole Walton, who supported me through the early stages of this book.

    To Allyn Roberts, Ph.D., a colleague and friend, who kindly read the book and added his valuable feedback.

    To Palma Richardson, Alice's daughter and a longtime friend, who generously provided input about the book.

    To all my sponsors and Twelve Step recovery friends.

    To Lee Lozowick and E. J. Gold, for their spiritual teachings.

    To Eric Brummel, a spiritual friend.

    To Spirit, River, Gracie and Migese, my four-legged companions, who were patient with me throughout the many hours I spent glued to the computer.

About the Author

Elaine A. Hodge holds a doctorate in educational psychology and counseling from the University of Cincinnati. She is a licensed psychologist in private practice in Prescott, Arizona. Previously, Dr. Hodge founded and directed the Holistic Center in Marquette, Michigan, and was associate professor of counseling at Northern Michigan University. She has also taught under-graduate psychology courses at Thomas More College and Yavapai College.

Dr. Hodge has had extensive post-doctoral training in human sexuality, alternative approaches to women's health, meditation, hypnosis, transpersonal psychotherapy, past life regression therapy, EMDR therapy, and body-mind therapies. She is certified by the International Board for Regression Therapy and the EMDR International Association. Hodge has taught seminars in Michigan and Arizona on human sexuality, rape prevention, self-empowerment, meditation, and spirituality.

Her articles have been published in the *Journal of Counseling Psychology* and *Harmony Bridge Magazine*. She is also the author of *Resource Manual for Rape*, which has been used at the Women's Center in Marquette, Michigan.

BOOKS

O is a symbol of the world, of oneness and unity. In different cultures it also means the "eye," symbolizing knowledge and insight. We aim to publish books that are accessible, constructive and that challenge accepted opinion, both that of academia and the "moral majority."

Our books are available in all good English language bookstores worldwide. If you don't see the book on the shelves ask the bookstore to order it for you, quoting the ISBN number and title. Alternatively you can order online (all major online retail sites carry our titles) or contact the distributor in the relevant country, listed on the copyright page.

See our website www.o-books.com for a full list of over 500 titles, growing by 100 a year.

And tune in to myspiritradio.com for our book review radio show, hosted by June-Elleni Laine, where you can listen to the authors discussing their books.